KINGDOM SHIFT

KINGDOM SHIFT

HOW TO PREPARE FOR GOD'S GLOBAL RESET

DEL HUNGERFORD

Available from www.amazon.com, www.healingfrequenciesmusic.com,
and other retail outlets where applicable.

ISBN: 978-1-7340956-1-6
Healing Frequencies Music Publications
Oldtown, ID 83822
USA
Special thanks to:
KingdomCovers.com for cover design and formatting
Lisa Thompson for editing
Dick Rabil for artwork and images

Contents

KINGDOM SHIFT

Introduction

I'm a regular person with a regular job and a regular life. One of my strongest character traits is a drive to persist. When I first understood that I could go to heaven before I die and participate in a real-time relationship with Yahweh (the Hebrew name for God), I pursued this concept with great fervor. Yahweh meets me where I am. He leads and I follow. He shows me and I do likewise. He loves me, and I learn to function through his love. The persistence he has instilled in me takes practice and perseverance.

In March of 2020, I attended a conference as a vendor. The day after the conference started, all the lockdowns began for COVID-19. I sat with my friend in our booth, and we joked that this situation might cause a global reset. As the speakers began to talk about a reset, my interest piqued. By the last day, a major shift into a new season had obviously begun.

Puzzle pieces began to drop into my spirit over the next few months as I questioned why the entire world shut down for a pandemic that has killed less people than the yearly flu. What was Yahweh showing us amid this circumstance? I already understood that according to ancient knowledge, the ages were shifting as we move out of Pisces and into Aquarius. Armed with questions and desiring to understand

Yahweh's will during a world-wide pandemic, I engaged the Trinity (Father, Son, and Holy Spirit) for a deeper understanding.

In the fall of 2020, many random puzzle pieces found their proper positions in the entrance to Aquarius puzzle. In a vision that transpired in an ancient document room in heaven, I saw some paperwork and was instructed to research and write this book. I focused on a recipe for functioning in a global reset, which requires stepping into a great awakening. When blinders are removed, we can experience what Yahweh has in store for us. We won't miss the bus because we can now see it.

This is a backwards book, starting with revelation first, then research. Father showed me the importance of seeing an age shift through his eyes, not my academic background. I researched the historical events that he indicated were important. From there, I received more revelation concerning the need for a great awakening. As I wrote, life examples flashed through my mind, reminding me of my own great awakening. Father instructed me to go through my journals and look for visions that provided perfect examples of stepping into the Age of Aquarius. As I reviewed the previous years of my life, I realized that key visions addressed this transition.

Every preconceived concept about how Yahweh works amid life situations was shattered during a seven-year period of my life while losing my home through the process of eminent domain. Understanding how to function in what I call the "come up here principle" helped me learn to truly see things through Father's eyes; a lot more is going on than I imagined. I now believe this situation propelled me into a greater understanding of how to function in a new season.

As I revisited my own encounters in the heavenly realms, I began reading my own stories from a perspective of how this fits into the process of stepping into a new age. A progression emerged. First, get into my position in Christ through developing a personal relationship with the Trinity. Second, understand how a shift in ages occurs from a historical perspective. Third, learn to see the transition through the Trinity's eyes where I am awakened to Yahweh's vision for the future. Fourth, step into truth and function in that truth as I partner with the Trinity in the creative process.

When I began this book, I had no idea where it would lead. After my research was completed for the first few chapters, I was then instructed to include some of my own stories. During the process of revisiting those visions, I understood why I needed to share specific encounters. Each story I chose was to focus on mankind's responsibility in creation, which can only be accomplished once we are awakened to that truth. Father instructed me to provide activations as practice opportunities to help others in their own transitions.

In school, teachers present facts first. As we experience the truths of those facts, they become a reality. As I wrote this book, Yahweh invited me to see how the last twenty years of my life prepared me for this shift in ages. The last twelve years involved the most intense schooling. Father enrolled me in kingdom school. I was awestruck by the concept that we are responsible for stewarding all of creation. Yahweh was faithful to walk beside me through my own personal great awakening.

I present the primary importance of our identity in Christ to be part of the creation process. All of creation groans until we wake up to our responsibilities. I provide the context for the shift into the Age of Aquarius, followed by examples from my own life. The activations offer practice opportunities as you walk through your own great awakening, which can propel you into functioning from your rightful position in Christ as we enter the Age of Aquarius. This is a why (teaching) and how (doing) book on preparing for the next great awakening as we learn to rule and reign as Sons of God in a new age.

PRELUDE

WELCOME TO MY world of interaction with the Trinity – Father (Yahweh), Son (Yeshua), and the Holy Spirit. What you read here may not line up with a current religious paradigm. Please keep an open mind and allow Holy Spirit to speak to you even in those places where something may be off your grid. Whenever I engage with the heavenlies, I ask questions about my encounters using a "Godly barometer checker." Those questions include: 1) Do the details within the encounter line up with the character of Yahweh? 2) Is what I'm seeing, sensing, hearing, and feeling bathed in Love? 3) Is anything required of me other than to love Yahweh and be loved by him? 4) Although a particular instance is not in the Bible, do my encounters line up with Biblical principles? 5) If something really does not make sense, when I look for any member of the Trinity in the experience, is one of them there?

I find that it's easier to write what comes to mind and judge it through Yahweh's character and the Word after I've written it all down. If I second guess myself, I often miss key points. It is important to note that when in an encounter, nothing will be asked of us other than to love and be loved. Yahweh never requires us to give or do something as an entrance point into his presence. There is no, "You need to do _____ before you get _____." Or "I'll show you _____ when you do _____."

After years of developing an intimate relationship with The Trinity, I can sense when they are near without having to see them. I have learned to recognize their frequency. If we go into any relationship with, "What's in it for me?" things often do not fare well for us in the end. Any intimate relationship requires equal give and take between all parties involved. In the heavenly encounters I share in this book, I learned what is on the heart of Yahweh and how to see life situations through his eyes. What I see is often totally opposite of my own beliefs about Yahweh and how he functions in a situation. There are times I have many questions and by sitting in his love and viewing a situation through his eyes, the answer comes.

This book is not about how to see in the spirit. If you are new to this, I recommend you first read "Accessing Your Spiritual Inheritance," written by myself and two other friends. My second book, "Accessing the Kingdom Realms," takes the relationship with Yahweh a step further where I share many of my personal experiences in the heavenly realms that brought me into a greater level of maturity. Both books are an introduction to learning how to function through a kingdom shift. We do that through what many call, "living the ascended lifestyle." We learn to live and function from a heavenly position where we see what Yahweh has to say about something as we look at what is happening on earth.

I came into the lifestyle of kingdom living believing I was a mature Christian. That belief was quickly thrown out the window when I realized many life traumas, incorrect religious paradigms, and reactions to life situations had yet to be resolved. If we hold onto hurts, grudges, play the victim, function out of fear, etc., this holds us back from going onto the next grade level of maturity in Kingdom School. We often do not realize it until a circumstance rears its ugly head and we respond out of what is in our hearts.

For example, let us look at fear as an issue of the heart. What is there to be fearful about? Responding with thoughts that go something like this, "If I don't wear a mask and others around me don't wear one, I could get COVID-19!" demonstrates how to function from a fearful position. My response is I don't "do" sick. My body is so infused with the love of Yahweh that no illness frequency can stand a chance of surviving in my body! That is what escorts fear out the door! When we align with Love, it resonates at a higher frequency, overriding fear.

I weigh what comes out of my mouth to determine what grade level I'm functioning from by paying attention to my first thoughts, feelings, and words. It has nothing to do with how much I know the Bible or walk a righteous lifestyle. "Accessing the Kingdom Realms" was my first step into a greater understanding of what is in my heart. The Word says that out of the abundance of the heart, the mouth speaks. (Luke 6:45) Until I began to live by the "come up here principle," (Rev. 4:1) I did not fully comprehend the meaning of this verse. When we add our thought life into the behavior recipe, thoughts lead to attitudes, which then create an action. The three work together to frame our world either negatively or positively. We are literally living out our thoughts, what we marinate in, and they become what we speak or act.

Our responses are examples of what comes up from the heart. Knee jerk reactions tell us a lot about the state of the heart. Out of the abundance of the heart, the mouth speaks and from that, an action follows. Let us look at COVID-19 as an example. Thinking back to the lockdowns, what was the first thought that came into your mind? How did you react those first few days and weeks? Many panicked, bought all the toilet paper in the stores and glared at anyone not wearing a mask. Others glued themselves to the news watching all the doom and gloom.

As you read this book, consider writing down anything that negatively triggers you. Take that before Yahweh and ask him what caused the trigger. As you are open to seeing a situation through his eyes, you may be surprised at the answer. Now, let's dig into the meat of the book

CHAPTER 1

THE ANCIENT DOCUMENT ROOM IN HEAVEN

A S I BEGAN research for this book, my intent was to step into revelation of a vision that occurred in a library in heaven. As an academic by trade, this point of view seems a bit backward to me, but when you think about it, Einstein and other great minds received most of their ideas through revelation. Many creatives don't understand where their revelation comes from. A perfect example of this type of mind is Mozart. He heard the music in his head, and all he had to do was write it down. He made minimal adjustments to his original manuscripts. Einstein would often play his violin for inspiration. For me, I focus on allowing Yahweh to teach me without an expectation of what an outcome should look like. It takes time to step into that position of intimacy with the Trinity. Relationship is relational. As it develops, understanding comes.

As I sat with Yahweh in an ancient document room in heaven, I looked over paperwork he set on the table before me. On the documents were titles with lists of information that explained each title. I conversed with him in real time concerning the materials you're about to read. At times, I watched my hands type as the words from Father scrolled through my thoughts, bypassing my intellect. I call this "real-time revelation."

I often step into the heavenlies and look to see where I am. I generally go with no agenda. However, in this case, a series of questions about current world events prompted the vision. Sometimes I receive answers right away. Other times, I don't have an aha moment for months or even years. In this encounter, Father waited for me, smiling at my inquisitiveness.

As I enter the room, I focus on the many books skillfully placed on the shelves in an ancient document section of a library in heaven. Many are bound with animal skins. Some appear thrown together with string-like threads connecting the pages. Others are simply rolled up scrolls written on parchment and animal hide. There are even cuneiform tablets, pictographs on slabs, and important writings on cave walls that were transferred to a recording device for storage in this room. I did not expect answers to my current event questions to be in this room.

I find myself with Yahweh in this large library. Although other rooms aren't visible, I understand this particular area is a room of ancient documents and wisdom in a larger library. Walls are covered with massive floor-to-ceiling deep-purple velvet curtains. The room has no lights even though it is well lit. The floor is a beautiful dark-chocolate-colored mahogany wood. Other walls are lined with books as far as the eye can see on very ornate wooden shelves—many never seen by man. Well, at least on earth.

In my spirit, as I peruse the books, I hear that books can be written on people's hearts. When people die and go to heaven, books in their hearts are finally written and are now in this room. In the center of the room is a giant oval-shaped wood table that can seat about twenty. Strewn across the top of the table are piles of paperwork waiting for me to sort. Yahweh sits across the table from me, pointing out key pages to investigate. At the top of each page is a title that describes the contents of the document.

What did I learn from this story?

I was instructed to write a book concerning what I saw in this ancient document room. Once I started the book, I realized that Yahweh began preparing me for this around 2015. I simply needed to assemble all the pieces to a puzzle. This book connects many of those puzzle pieces.

Through heavenly encounters, I met with various individuals in the cloud of witnesses as well as the Trinity on this journey. The cloud of witnesses includes those who have passed on before us that are now in heaven. Part of their job is to help us fulfill our destinies on earth. I've found that many are more than willing to share their mistakes so I can learn from them. In this book, I introduce those in the cloud of witnesses who assist me on this journey into sonship. Sonship refers to mankind's relationship with the Trinity. In these encounters, I first learned to pay attention to cycles and patterns.

What can you learn from this story?

If this challenges any religious thinking, that's probably a positive thing. I found that when I wasn't challenged, I could too easily walk in deception. As you continue to read this book, I encourage you to do the following:

Any time fear presents itself, ask Yahweh what's causing it.

Anytime a belief system is challenged, ask Yahweh to show you his truth.

If you read anything that goes against what you've been taught, ask Yahweh to show you his truth.

If something doesn't make sense, set it aside and allow Yahweh to speak to you over time. I find that when I do this, he unpacks the mystery as I mature in my personal relationship with him.

Practice the activations at the end of the various chapters. They are meant to assist you in learning how to function in a reset that leads to your own personal great awakening.

Consider setting the book down when one of these five points grabs your attention. Ponder on the following. Immediately see yourself sitting with the Trinity. Allow love to flow through you. As you do this, receive Yahweh's heart on the matter. Marinate in his love, making it a part of your being as you continue to read. Put whatever doesn't make sense on a shelf and wait for a revealing of the understanding. You may also step into an experience and see for yourself. Use my experiences as a springboard for your own.

Later in the book, I talk about the great awakening, which is a necessary part of the process. In fact, without a personal great awakening, you will struggle to fully embrace this next season. This book is part of my personal great awakening because I began to see my identity in Christ from a higher dimensional position. I underwent a paradigm shift where I had to understand and grasp the importance of mankind's role on Earth. When we take the enormity of this concept to heart, our attitudes and actions might even change our planet and the cosmos. Imagine what that would look like. If this concept is new to you, welcome to your first great awakening.

We move next to discovering more about our identity in Christ. Mankind's role in creation as well as restoration is a key mandate for the Sons of Yahweh (mankind).

CHAPTER 2

THE EARTH RESPONDS TO OUR IDENTITY

TO BETTER UNDERSTAND our identity in Christ at a deeper level, we must realize that we are given a mandate to participate in the creation and restoration process. This concept is critical to learn how to rule and reign as Sons of Yahweh in the Age of Aquarius. Our identity is extremely important in how we function in a great awakening. Nothing else will fall into its proper order until we see that co-creating with Christ is part of our identity.

In my time with him in the ancient document room, Yahweh invited me to connect several puzzle pieces as we enter this global reset. Simply put, we're entering a new age—the Age of Aquarius. We have a role to play, which involves functioning through our position and identity in Christ. From that position, we release, legislate, decree, declare, and foster an attitude of peace and love. The position we take affects the entirety of creation and how it responds.

For years, I functioned from head knowledge concerning my identity in him. I had to practice a lot to move from my head to my heart. How do I know that? My behavior proved it. Our immediate reactions to situations demonstrate what realm we operate from. When we function in Christ, we react with love, peace, joy, kindness, patience, goodness, etc. The first thoughts and actions that well up within us determine how far we are in the process. It's a journey. We make mistakes, so the only way to keep going forward is to continually run the race. When we fall, get back up. As long as our eyes are focused on Yeshua, our falls have less debilitating effects on our psyche.

Humanity is responsible for all of creation. Romans 8:19 says that all creation groans for the revealing of the Sons of Yahweh. What does that really mean? Biblewheel.com provides an English-to-Greek comparison with links to the meanings of the words in *The Strong's Concordance*. That same verse in the King James Version from Biblewheel.com says, "For the earnest expectation of the creature waiteth for the manifestation of the sons of God."[1]

The Greek word for the phrase "the earnest expectation" is αποκαραδοκια (apokaradokia). It comes from Strong's 575 and is a compound of kara (the head).[2] Strong's 1380 (in the sense of watching) refers to earnest expectation or anxious and persistent expectation.[3]

"Of the creature" is the Greek word κτισις (ktisis) and comes from Strong's 2936, meaning "creature, creation, building, or ordinance."[4] It's the act of creating individual things, beings, creatures, or creation itself. As Sons of Yahweh, we are part of the creation process. Adam and Eve were called to take care of creation and, although they messed it up, the mandate still exists. That responsibility is now upon us, the Sons of Yahweh.

The next phrase, "for the manifestation," is the Greek word αποκαλυψις (apokalupsis). It comes from Strong's 601, meaning "revelation, be revealed, or to lighten."[5] It can also be a manifestation, coming, appearing, a laying bare, making naked, a disclosure of truth, instruction, or concerning things before unknown. Apokalupsis is also used when things, states, or persons withdrawn from view are made visible to all as in a manifestation or appearance.

The final word, "sons," is taken from the Greek word υιος (huios).[6] Although the list of meanings is quite long, the basic meaning of huios refers to humans as Yahweh's sons as opposed to animals. We are called to rule and reign over creation, taking dominion over it, and treating it with honor, all while functioning through Yahweh's love.

When taking this Scripture and unpacking it, we find that it might better read, "with earnest and persistent expectation, creation itself eagerly and expectantly waits for Yahweh's sons (the human race) to disclose the truth of *who they are* for the purpose of continuing the creation process." This verse calls us to walk in our identity as Sons of Yahweh. In the meantime, creation (the entire cosmos) groans until we step into the position Adam and Eve left open because of their choices. Adam and Eve let go of stewarding creation. Just because they stepped away from that responsibility doesn't mean we have to as well. Let that truth sink it.

Romans 8:23 says, "Not only so, but we ourselves, who have the firstfruits of the Spirit, groan inwardly as we wait eagerly for our adoption to sonship, the redemption of our bodies." This includes mankind in that we, as Sons of Yahweh, also groan as we step into who are called to be. Our bodies take some time to catch up with the reality of who we are. As we continually work out the bugs in our lives, what's inside us flows to all creation so that its groaning responds to our level of sonship. You'll see how this works when I share how Yeshua has me breathe on the stars.

In Genesis 1:28, we read that "God blessed them [mankind] and said to them, 'Be fruitful and increase in number; fill the earth and subdue it. Rule over the fish in the sea and the birds in the sky and over every living creature that moves on the ground.'" "Subdue" comes from the Hebrew word, שבכ *kabash*. It means "to subdue, bring into subjection, bring into bondage, or make subservient." "Rule" is the Hebrew word, הדר *radah*. It also means "to rule, take dominion, prevail, be a ruler, have dominion, or dominate."[7]

When we don't participate in the creation process, a waiting and longing occurs. Waiting has a sound—a frequency. Some translations show this by inserting the word "groaning." When something groans, it's calling for help. Earth groans until Yahweh's sons step into the original mandate of caring for, nurturing, and taking dominion over creation. When we're not following our path of destiny, the entire formula is thrown off. Creation responds to our stress, fear, anxiety, etc. Natural disasters, civil unrest, plagues, and famines are a direct result of how mankind stewards creation. We'll see how and why that works in an upcoming chapter.

When we function from a negative state of being (poor identity), the universe responds to our negative energy. When we don't live according to the original mandate given to mankind, it's as if we let a house go without repairs for so many years that it eventually caves in on itself. Caring for the earth is more than being a tree hugger or practicing green living. It's about honoring all of creation, including each other. When we're arguing and fighting, the earth responds to those negative frequencies via natural occurrences. Negative responds to negative. When our lives are full of negativity, we're also functioning in a poor identity.

For each age or, as I describe in a later chapter, for the entrance to each great month, we have an opportunity to shift back to our original call. Should we choose to accept the mission, we learn more about our identity. As the changing of an age approaches, the earth groans louder. We see that through turmoil on the land, civil unrest within people groups, and natural phenomenon, such as earthquakes, volcanos, etc. We wonder why there are so many natural disasters. Chaos takes over when we can't control ourselves. As we enter the Age of Aquarius, we're once again given the opportunity to step into our mandate as Sons of Yahweh. Will we recognize and step into that call?

This is a call to a great awakening. For creation to respond as intended, the Sons of Yahweh must arise and become who we were created to be from the beginning of time. Creation answers the call as the Sons of Yahweh take their rightful place by governing through Yahweh's love. Through building an intimate relationship with the Trinity, my eyes opened to see how creation responds to what I do, what I say, how I treat others, how I care for myself, and how I govern creation itself. This was my first personal great awakening. The frequency that I resonate flows beyond me, affecting the creation within my sphere of influence. As I mature, that sphere extends further and further.

My process of stepping into a greater truth of my identity began once I realized that I didn't have to die before going to heaven. We can function simultaneously from heaven and Earth when we walk in relationship with the Trinity. I stepped away from looking to prophets, apostles, and teachers and instead sought the Lord for direction from him. Now, those words and teachings confirm what Yahweh shows me. From this heavenly position, Yahweh introduced me to my role in creation.

We need to awaken to mankind's role and take authority as governors over the entire universe. We do that by looking at how we functioned for the past 2,500 years and how the Earth and heavens responded to our stewardship over creation. That sets a gauge for where we are currently positioned, so we learn from our mistakes as we enter the Age of Aquarius. We do this through a personal great awakening.

CHAPTER 3

A GREAT AWAKENING

WE MUST HAVE a great awakening regarding our role as Sons of God by understanding that we are to steward all of creation. We can't do that unless we first understand our position in Christ at a deeper level. Looking back in history, we see evidence of this process in the Great Awakening that began in the 1730s.

How do great awakenings begin? Wars, civil uprisings, and resets of entire nations often precede great awakenings. The catalyst to start the process is a desire for people to worship their god of choice (freedom of religious choice), especially when they feel oppressed. This happened when the great awakening began in the early 1730s. Amid civil unrest due to opposing ideas, the instigators desired to bring the truth of who Yahweh is to the people. A great awakening is part of a global reset recipe. However, until we're awakened, we can miss details because they don't line up with our current paradigms.

One writer provides a simple description of the first Great Awakening.

During the First Great Awakening, evangelists came from the ranks of several Protestant denominations: Congregationalists, Anglicans (members of the Church of England), and Presbyterians. They rejected what appeared to be sterile, formal modes of worship in favor of a vigorous emotional religiosity. Whereas Martin Luther and John Calvin had preached a doctrine of predestination and close reading of Scripture, new evangelical ministers spread a message of personal and experiential faith that rose above mere book learning. Individuals could bring about their own salvation by accepting Christ, an especially welcome message for those who had felt excluded by traditional Protestantism: women, the young, and people at the lower end of the social spectrum.[8]

At the opposite end of the spectrum, the Age of Enlightenment (Age of Reason) coincided with the Great Awakening, which focused on reason and science over blind faith and superstition. Enlightenment was in direct opposition to the Great Awakening, which set the stage for division. Civil unrest starts as an unwillingness to see something from another's perspective. In most cases, it infringes on freedoms, which sets off unrest. We also see a shift in religious thinking along with civil unrest at the time of Christ. This mirrors our current state of affairs.

The New Age movement that began in the 1950s was similar to the Age of Reason. It's about self—what I can do within myself so I can become a better person. The modern New Age movement is basically a replica of the Age of Reason. Both are the direct opposite of Yahweh's plan even though some of the ideas are accurate. Much of the material in the New Age movement comes directly from Scripture. But the material is twisted because it's about self rather than about a relationship with the One who created us.

An entrance into each new season (or new age) appears to coincide with some form of religious awakening due to opposition of current religious freedoms. We see that at the time Christ was born, in the 1700s and 2000s. These awakenings change how we view religion and religious activities. They also change how we function in life and how we look at relationships with other people.

Historically, only the rabbis and other educated religious leaders could read religious writings. The common people had to go through one who was deemed close enough to Yahweh for their spiritual food. Even in the great awakening movements, the focus was still on great teachers and what they brought to the table. It was a time of fiery passion in preaching that used fear to tug on people's heartstrings: If you don't repent, you'll go to hell. Many followed the teachers instead of coming closer to Yahweh on their own because that was their paradigm. This move transitioned from trained ministers in the church to anointed lay people not necessarily sanctioned by any church. Many manifested signs and wonders.

Signs and wonders attracted people. We see this in the charismatic and healing movements of the mid-twentieth century. People expected tangible manifestations of God's glory. Yet again, the idea of a personal relationship with Yahweh was lost to the masses. Looking back in history, we see it's a repeat of what occurred in Yeshua's time. People were more interested in the signs and wonders than in understanding the truth that Yeshua preached.

Many call the time after Christ's death the church age—the Age of Pisces as represented by the fish symbol in Christianity. Constantine is responsible for our current church model. We're taught that you find Yahweh in church, Bible study, or other religious gatherings. You go to a building with a group of people, worship, say a few prayers, take an offering, listen to a preacher, meet and greet all your friends, and hopefully practice what you learned in the sermon during the week. But I'm not convinced Yahweh had this model in mind because it puts Yahweh in a box when we dictate how we want him to move in our services. When disagreements over doctrine or church practices occur, people leave to start other churches or denominations.

Many religious leaders since the early 2000s described an upcoming major shift from our standard church model. COVID-19 seemed to speed up that shift by not allowing religious gatherings or worship, specifically singing. The church is currently fighting for its very existence. But maybe it's time to let go of what we've considered sacred. Have we ever considered that Yahweh may be using the current world situation to show us a new way? This doesn't mean that Yahweh creates pandemics. It means he uses circumstances to help us grow and learn. I demonstrate how that works through the loss of my home to eminent domain in the final chapters of this book. We must allow Yahweh to speak to our open hearts, putting aside expectations of what we think and expect change to look like.

We must step away from church doctrine into a personal relationship with Yahweh. However, over the last one hundred years, we became completely stuck in the model of who we are submitting to. Have we ever considered that this is not how Yahweh wants us to operate? Yeshua paid the price for our sins on the cross. His life, death, and resurrection created a direct pathway for us to connect with Yahweh. The curtain in the temple ripped in half. This prophetic act showed Yahweh's people that we no longer need a priest to enter the holy of holies on our behalf. We are to step into that intimate relationship ourselves without the aid of someone we're required to submit to. Our covering should be Yahweh, not our pastor.

People in our current culture obviously want governmental agencies and religious organizations to care for them with free health care, free college, free food, free everything. But this mentality transfers our desire to earthly governments, including church government. Yes, the church should take care of the poor, the widows, and those who are struggling. On the other hand, church leadership has taken this to a higher level of control. The standard church model looks something like this.

- The people submit to a minister or pastor.
- The pastor submits to a board of directors or denominational set of standards.

- The minister often determines how we are to function in the church as well as how we are to live our lives. We receive minimal encouragement to think for ourselves.
- We expect the preacher to tell us everything we need to know.

We've become so spoon-fed that we can only function when given step-by-step instructions. This is a direct result of our expectation that someone more spiritual than us is better equipped to know and understand Yahweh's will for us. So we run to prophets and apostles to find the will of the Lord. But we can go directly to Yahweh ourselves without the need for a pastor or senior leader to confirm that we've heard the voice of the Lord. As we step into a deeper understanding of our identity in Christ, we are awakened to the truth about our responsibility as Sons of Yahweh.

How can we step into greater personal responsibility in our relationship with Yahweh? Why do we seem to rely on teachers as our main source of information for greater spiritual understanding? I can hear the question now, "What if I'm deceived?" Deception is fear. Fear is not of Yahweh. Building a personal relationship with Yahweh is the same as having a best friend. If we are concerned about deception, consider the five questions I presented in the introduction as a plumb line to check what we are hearing with Yahweh's character.

When we learn to take that leap of faith into a new paradigm of what church looks like, we may be on our way to the next great awakening. Part of an awakening involves spending personal time with the Trinity daily so we're not relying on the most recent prophetic words or teachings to direct us.

I can't tell you what it will look like as we enter the Age of Aquarius, nor should I. You'd then be following my ideas, not Yahweh's. Should we choose to accept our new mission, we can learn that kingdom living is experiential and relational rather than an I-teach-and-you-regurgitate-back-to-me model that we've become so accustomed to. The best teachers invite us into experiential learning. That's what Yeshua did with the disciples.

I don't believe the new look of the church will be single-leader based. We all have a responsibility to participate in the process. First, step into your personal identity in Christ at a deeper level. Understand that you are part of the process, not a passive onlooker. Second, bring something to the table when you meet with others. Don't always expect someone to spiritually feed you. Activate and foster your own relationship with Yahweh and be prepared to help mentor others that aren't as far along as you are. This next great awakening focuses on a greater responsibility to steward all of creation, learn to function through ascension (the come-up-here principle) as standard operating procedure, and to do everything from a position of love in Christ.

In the next two chapters, we look at points in history where we see patterns on a timeline for major shifts from one season to the next. It's a bit academic in nature, so bear with me as I present background on key important points. We'll compare how these patterns repeat as we transition from each great year and great month. Everything in creation functions on a cyclical pattern. We see this in the changing of a season: month-to-month and year-to-year.

CHAPTER 4

THE GREAT YEAR AND GREAT MONTH

WHEN WE STEP into our role as part of the creation process with Christ, we need to understand how creation functions. Historical context helps provide keys to this puzzle. In the next two chapters, we explore cyclical patterns in the cosmos and in history that outline key components of shifting from one age to the next.

What are the great year and the great month? How do they affect where we're moving over the next few years? We'll start with a definition. "The Great Year is the term that some ancient civilizations use to describe the slow precession of the equinox through the twelve houses of the ancient zodiac, a period that takes about 24,000 years." [9] The earth rotates counter-clockwise in a wobble, so it moves through the zodiac houses in reverse order.

The great year is made up of the twelve zodiacal great months, each about 2,160 years for a total of somewhere around 25,920 years. The great year is so named because it takes the earth that long to complete the rotational wobble and arrive back in the same position where it started. On the wobble journey, the earth passes through each of the zodiacal houses (a great month), phasing out of one and into another. Two great months overlap; one finishes as the new month arrives on the scene. Anywhere from two hundred to six hundred years can pass before the shift occurs. Those who watch the signs in the heavens come up with many theories for starting and ending dates for every great month. However, there is no hard and fast rule.

Many events occur during transitions from one great month to the next. These events may include natural disasters, wars, civil unrest, changes in paradigms, creativity, enlightenment, expanded knowledge, famines, illness, etc. In my vision, I was specifically instructed to pay attention to plagues, famines, and other natural events. The paperwork on the table in the library of heaven was lined with these headings, so I knew what to look for.

I found many opinions on how to map out the great year. Some were scientific and others more spiritual. A consensus seems to be that it takes just under 26,000 years to complete one great year with the twelve great months somewhat equally divided although some are slightly longer than others. We are currently near the end of Pisces. Some experts say Pisces is a little longer year than the following year, Aquarius. Soon, Aquarius will be in full swing, and Pisces won't come around again for another 25,920 years.

The ancients identified the change in great months by watching the skies. When certain stars and planets aligned, the astronomers and astrologers of the time knew that the great month had advanced. This applies to the birth of Yeshua as the magi from the east knew exactly when that special birth would happen. The moment the stars aligned correctly, they set off with gifts for the baby Jesus. These wise men understood how to read the signs in the heavens. The magi appeared to understand the heavenly message to know when to seek out the baby Jesus.

Frances Rolleston wrote *Mazzaroth, or the Constellations* in 1862. In the book, she outlines how the twelve constellations tell the gospel message. One of the best descriptions of the book is found on Google books.

> Modern biblical dictionaries and commentaries designed for a popular readership tend to shy away from any reference to the word Mazzaroth, let alone attempt to interpret it. This is scarcely surprising, for the word is obscure, and it occurs only once in the Bible; twice, if it is equated with Mazzaloth. Traditional sources tended to interpret the word as meaning the constellations, specifically those forming the zodiac. But there was no universal agreement; others accepted that the word referred to the zodiac or even identified it with the star Sirius. The idiosyncratic ideas expressed in the four parts of Mazzaroth and its appendix Mizraim, are all based on solid research—misapplied, perhaps, in light of Rolleston's steadfast Christian outlook, but fully documented and with sources quoted at length. The whole work provides the reader with an amazing compendium of obscure material on ancient mythology, symbolism, and etymology, with comprehensive biblical references and a wealth of learned and detailed footnotes. Much of the information is set out in a tabular form that inevitably reminds the reader of S. L. MacGregor Mathers's book of correspondences that we know as 777. And this may not be coincidental. Mazzaroth may have been passed over by reviewers when it appeared, but it was not ignored by esoteric scholars, even though they were not its intended readership. W. Wynn Westcott possessed a copy and loaned it to the Golden Dawn library, where it was certainly read by F. L. Gardner (he includes the book, albeit misdated, in his Bibliotheca Astrologica) and most probably by Mathers when he compiled 777. It is a valuable resource that fully deserves its rescue from oblivion, just as its neglected author deserves our praise.

Rolleston (1781–1864) spent her life studying the sky and the Scriptures.[10]

In order to understand how cyclical patterns affect everything on earth, we must take a walk down history lane and peruse various global resets that occur at the changing of an age from one great month to the next. I didn't research the history of every change over the last twenty-five thousand years, but I did look at the transition into Pisces (around 500 BC) through the transition into Aquarius (around AD 1770). A quick survey of ages further back revealed that major natural events occurred right around the passage from one age to the next. As a reminder, the ages move through the zodiacal houses in reverse order because the earth's rotational wobble is counter-clockwise.

Pythagoras and Plato came on the scene during the great month of Pisces. This was a time of great creativity, amazing advances in the earlier sciences, enlightenment, and progress toward education. Based on what I saw in the paperwork on the library table, I knew to look up more than human happenings. I came up with a rubric of sorts. I looked for major weather events (beyond seasonal); an increase of civil wars and unrest as one great month entered the next; and pandemics, famines, droughts, earthquakes, volcanoes, and other natural disasters that weren't brought on by humans. I also looked at other major events that changed paradigms.

As Aries began the transition into Pisces, Pythagoras and other learned men began to teach how the heavens and earth were connected. Around 1 AD, Yeshua was born. That brought the beginning of Christianity and the end of the age of Aries. Many believe that this time in history was the infancy of Pisces. As we move from Pisces to Aquarius, we're seeing repeated patterns that mirror earlier age changes.

The Christian fish symbol represents the age of Pisces. Many astrologers and astronomers say Pisces is the Christian age and that we're moving out of it. World events, especially droughts and famines, are all about water as we travel into Aquarius. We're moving from a dry place into a fertile season that promotes growth. The hippies in the 1960s understood that the age of Aquarius quickly approaches. To see what's involved with that change, we begin our journey into historical events.

CHAPTER 5

A WALK DOWN HISTORY LANE

E ACH GREAT MONTH flows into the next, taking about two hundred to six hundred years for a full transition. We can see that as Pisces takes the stage around 400 to 500 BC through when Aries finally let go, probably by AD 100. There are differences of opinion on the starting date of Pisces, but you can pinpoint the date more closely based on historical events by considering several factors. In my encounters with Yahweh, my assignment was to look for patterns in history. When patterns emerge, answers present themselves. You'll see them during transitions in and out of each age.

Key points I considered for this book focus on increased occurrences of life-changing events at entrances and exits from one age to the next. I saw these titles on the paperwork in the ancient document room:
- civil wars and unrest[11]
- pandemics[12]
- famines[13]
- droughts[14]

- earthquakes[15]
- volcanoes[1617]
- other non-seasonal natural disasters that weren't brought on by humans and
- other major event(s) that caused a paradigm shift in human behavior and thinking

Excess rain, floods, tornados, typhoons, wildfires, and hurricanes weren't considered as individual occurrences because they are too numerous across the timeline and often fit within seasonal patterns. Floods are often caused by tsunamis, which are triggered by earthquakes. Many natural disasters work together to create a series of events. As an example, I found four or five natural disasters within a short period of time that led to drought, which then led to famine. My strategy was to peruse the overall picture, looking for inconsistencies and periods on the timeline where events were amplified and affected greater land areas and people.[18]

If the transition into Pisces began somewhere between BC 400–500, let us run through my list of occurrences. First of all, is there a major paradigm shift in human progress? The answer to that is a definite yes. It was the time of great thinkers, such as Pythagoras and Plato. It appeared to be a move from mythology to scientific thinking and of the function of the heavens and earth as a unit. Next, Rome ruled most of the world, and many were tired of that control. Between 1–100 AD, we not only see an increase in earthquakes but greater civil unrest. Yeshua's birth, death, and resurrection created major religious paradigm shifts that may have been the final push into the age of Pisces. Three major events contributed to lasting change.

To test my theory, I put together a list of all the major events from BC 500–2020 AD. Figure 1 lists what years various incidences occurred. Civil unrest and wars aren't included for the same reason seasonal weather patterns aren't included; they are too numerous and occur fairly regularly throughout every age. However, a spike in civil unrest is seen at the very tail end of Aries before Pisces is fully established and then again as Pisces settles in. This is similar to the events leading up to 2020 where we're leaving Pisces and entering Aquarius.

Figure 1 — Natural Events 500 BCE – 2020 AD

YEARS	EARTHQUAKES	VOLCANOES	DROUGHTS FAMINES	PLAGUES OUTBREAKS	WORLDWIDE PANDEMICS	TOTALS
Transition – Aries to Pisces 500 BCE-100AD						
500 – 0 BCE	4	4	1	1	0	10
Aries ends 1 – 100	8	4	1	unknown	0	10

Significant Events During Transition: Life of Jesus; Fall of Jerusalem 70AD; Christian Church Age begins

YEARS	EARTHQUAKES	VOLCANOES	DROUGHTS FAMINES	PLAGUES OUTBREAKS	WORLDWIDE PANDEMICS	TOTALS
Age of Pisces 101-1770 AD						
Age of Pisces 101 – 1770 AD	6	22	147	71	0	246

Significant Events During the Age: End of Roman Empire; Christian Church is prominent; Discovery of America; Renaissance

YEARS	EARTHQUAKES	VOLCANOES	DROUGHTS FAMINES	PLAGUES OUTBREAKS	WORLDWIDE PANDEMICS	TOTALS
Transition – Pisces to Aquarius 1770-Present						
Transition Begins: 1770 – 1800	1	5	12	9	0	27
Transition 2: 1801 – 1850	3	4	15	24	1	47
Transition 3: 1851 – 1900	2	6	21	30	2	61
Transition 4: 1901 – 1950	8	8	41	18	3	78
Transition 5: 1951 – 2000	15	18	20	17	4	74
Pisces Ending: 2001 – Present	14	12	24	60	6	116

Significant Events During Transition: United States of America formed; Great Awakenings (AZUSA Street); Industrial Revolution; Science & Technology Discoveries; Moon Landing; Wealth Creation; COVID 19 Pandemic

	TOTALS
Aries to Pisces Transition Total Events (600 years)	20
Age of Pisces Total Events (1,669 years)	246
Pisces to Aquarius Transition Total Events (250 years)	403

The chart sets the transition from Aries to Pisces at six hundred years. The next large chunk of dates on the timeline is the walking out of Pisces, which lasts another 1669 years. From the start of the transition to the end of Pisces, Pisces appears to be about 2,277 years as it flows into Aquarius around 1770. Why does this period in history stand out? We look for important events that eventually have a world-wide impact. First, America declared its independence from Britain and began the process of becoming a separate country. The US's bid for independence started a new wave of progress and thinking. When considering all possible incidences during Pisces, the events of the 1770s most fit my criteria as the transition point: (1) a major and long-lasting paradigm shift in human thinking, (2) exponential increase of civil unrest or political change and/or a shift in religious paradigms, and (3) an increase in natural disasters, plagues, and famines.

Let's use circa 1770 as the beginning of a transition from Pisces into Aquarius. With the formula set up earlier, we see several major shifts. The second major catalyst to worldwide change was the beginning of the industrial revolution in 1760 that continued into the 1820s. The United States and Europe worked on new processes of manufacturing that brought worldwide scientific and technological breakthrough. This was the beginning of the technology era.[19]

The third event, the Great Awakening, began in the 1730s with four separate Christian awakenings that continued into the late twentieth century. A greater interest in a personal relationship with Yahweh brought many new denominations and a religious fervor that hadn't been seen in years. These awakenings changed the face of the church and how it functioned. They set up a current shift in the twenty-first century from the church age to the kingdom age where we're learning to function as Sons of Yahweh from a heavenly rather than earthly perspective. This next change takes our relationship with Yahweh to a deeper level.[20]

When reviewing events between 100 and 1770 AD, we don't see these types of worldwide events that brought about long-lasting behavioral changes. When Yeshua was born, his life changed religion as we know it. When America became a country, she soon positioned herself as a world leader. The Great Awakening had much to do with the settling of the US. We can obviously see this when we read the country's constitution.

As a recap, three major events around the year 1770 led to world-wide paradigm shifts. Adjustments in long-lasting belief systems, technology, art, science, etc. appear to be a clue to a shift between ages. These events pinpoint a transition from Pisces into the Age of Aquarius: the process of the great awakenings, the industrial revolution, and the establishment of the US as its own country.

A rise in civil unrest also indicates a transition between ages. To put it bluntly, civil unrest often begins when people want their own way and can't see other views. Those in power force their views on others, opening the door for a series of reactions and rebellions. In some cases, civil unrest starts because of government oppression. The government then uses violence to instill fear, hoping the perceived fear will result in a desired outcome. This is evident with all the governmental turmoil during the life of Christ and after his death. We see this in current events with the destructive riots in various cities around the world during COVID-19, especially in the US. Rioters want the government to cave to their demands. So we see civil unrest in three forms: government control, those not in government who want control, and those who are oppressed by a government and who want to escape the control.

Another indicator of a move to a new age is an increase in natural disasters, plagues, famines, droughts, etc. From 100 to 1770 AD, the entire range of dates includes only 246 events over 1,600 years. That number may eventually change as archaeology, ancient writings, and science bring new events to light. We begin to see an increase in various disasters around the year 1770. From 1770 to 2020, a total of

403 events span only 250 years. That's a major increase in worldwide instances in a relatively short period of time.

Look at the pandemics, plagues, and sicknesses in Figure 1. They exponentially increase as we approach the year 2020. With modern medicine, one would expect those numbers to decrease. Maybe modern medicine isn't what it's cracked up to be, or other factors are at work here. Many of the plagues and illnesses over the course of time are caused by weather changes, such as drought, too much rain, too much heat, etc. Other illnesses are brought on by wars and famine. In the twentieth century alone, there were two world wars. Those wars led to worldwide famine, economy crashes, and civil unrest. In the twenty-first century, we see double the numbers in half the time. Is it possible these are clues to the entrance of the Age of Aquarius?

Interestingly, the first worldwide pandemic isn't mentioned until the year 1847. Then we see an increase in the number of pandemics from one every fifty years to six pandemics in a nineteen-year timespan. As I write this at the end of 2020, COVID-19 has shut down the entire world for nearly a full year. This pandemic is bringing civil unrest—an unrest that's brewed under the surface for many years and finally popped its cork when the going got tough. With all this evidence, we appear to have nearly transitioned out of Pisces and into Aquarius, possibly as soon as spring 2021.

Many are saying that the global reset began during the current pandemic. From a historical point of view, a reset involves a major great awakening. If we are indeed entering the Age of Aquarius, we need to learn how to function even when civil unrest stares us in the face. Since few know what this next season holds, we're all essentially infants learning how to function in the unknown. Parents (the Trinity) show us the way. As we follow by example, we mature into who we are meant to be. This takes us back to the chapter on our identity. When we understand our true identity, we walk out our book of instructions for living life. We are at a unique position in history where we can either grasp the change and move forward or turn around and repeat history.

If we don't learn from our past, we're destined to repeat it. As we enter the age of Aquarius, will we step fully into it or be driven back by a fear of the unknown? Will a fear of deception cripple us? For religious people, a fear of deception leads to deception. It's time to step out of our comfortable boxes and see what Yahweh has for us. For many, this requires a leap of faith into the heart of Yahweh as he leads like a parent into the new and wonderful things yet ahead for us. Will we take that leap of faith? Will we stay in the place of rest and allow the Trinity to teach us what this next age looks like? Can we stay in a place of love in the heart of the Father, no matter what goes on around us? Remember, each age seems to bring a new level of religious thinking. I believe we're exiting the church age and entering something that will look very different than church on Sunday morning. Are we ready for that?

CHAPTER 6

How to Prepare for a Great Awakening

MOVING INTO A new season requires paradigm changes and letting go of religious thinking that keeps us in a box. The shapes and sizes of those boxes are determined by how we were raised, what we were taught, and what we chose to believe. The more ingrained a belief system is, the more difficult it can be for us to realize we're in that place. Changing a belief system requires experience and practice of a new paradigm. Some situations along the way will challenge everything we've ever believed. COVID-19 is a perfect example. During this global reset, we have an opportunity to step into Yahweh's reset. Yes, there is a counterfeit but we aren't focusing on that. Yahweh is bigger than the enemy's plan. We saw that as Yeshua was crucified. The enemy thought he won. Well, we all know how that turned out.

If you're in a place where this is new to you, consider connecting with groups that are engaging with this process. I'll list those at the end of the book. Although I began this journey alone, I understand that it's helpful to have others alongside you. The key in this age shift is to stay in a place of peace and rest without putting too much emphasis on the world happenings around us. Yes, we live among them, but they don't have to rule us. Imagine if the entire world decided to respond out of love rather than out of hate and fear. The world would look vastly different than it does now.

Entering a new age generally means starting from an infant stage. Why? Because we don't know how to function in it yet. Infants have no clue how to do anything. Parents do everything for them. As we step into Aquarius, those who have a certain level of maturity may assist in leading us in, even if they may be only one step ahead of the rest of us. But God! When we step into a position of relationship with Yahweh, he will show us the way. For that to work properly, we'll need to let go of our pet theories and preconceived ideas. I can't stress this enough. The bottom line is that we are leaving the church age and are in the process of new great awakening.

How do we prepare for a great awakening? A major key is to constantly be aware of our first reactions. I previously suggested that we consider our knee-jerk reactions. Those are the first thoughts that come into our brain the moment something happens. Those thoughts come from our hearts. Remember, out of the abundance of the heart, the mouth speaks. (See Luke 6:45.)

Next, ask the question, "Yahweh, what beliefs have I held that aren't of you? What am I carrying that no longer serves your purpose?" When I ask these questions, I ascend into the heavenly realms, sit with members of the Trinity, and allow them to show me their ways. Those ways are often different than what I was taught. Experience leads to understanding. WARNING! Don't ask this question unless you really want to know the answer.

Consider these suggestions in preparation for a personal great awakening.

- Allow Yahweh to lead you. Consider prophecies and teachings but don't allow them to guide you *in place of* personal interaction with the Trinity.

- Don't look to the right or left. Keep your eyes on Yahweh the entire time despite the circumstances.
- Learn to see everything through the eyes of Yahweh from a position of love. See people who treat us poorly or governmental leaders that make interesting decisions through Yahweh's love filter.
- Don't allow circumstances to rule your emotions.
- Stay in a place of rest and peace, no matter what happens.
- Keep short accounts.
- Repent and forgive as needed. Repentance keeps the enemy at bay so that emotions don't fester into something more harmful.
- Step into childlike faith and trust Yahweh's plan despite what you see. You can participate in his plan through understanding his heart for the entire cosmos. Then do your part to facilitate that plan.
- Learn to step into the presence of Yahweh to see and understand his plans.
- When you mess up or make a mistake, get back up and start again.
- Learn to live an ascended lifestyle of living in Christ all day, every day. I call it the come-up-here principle. This is more of an attitude than trying to do it. Like everything else, it takes practice.
- Learn to act based on Yahweh's direction, not on your emotions or on what head knowledge suggests.
- Go to the Trinity to get their heart on a matter.
- When you are given an assignment from the Trinity, step into the assignment despite reasonings, feelings, personal desires, and emotions.
- Be careful what you watch, what you listen to, how much time you spend around negativity, and what you read. Do these activities produce life or death?
- Choose life.

As we purpose to step into Yahweh's plan for this next age, we must deal with the issues in our lives that hold us back. This may involve healing sessions, mentoring, and working with those we trust to help us on our journey. We will no longer be able to function in business as usual as we step out of the standard church model. A new age requires a new mindset. We often go through an uncomfortable stage before we're willing to let go. It's okay to be uncomfortable. Don't be surprised if you see some of that occurring in your own life. If your focus is on seeing situations through Yahweh's eyes despite what you expect, you're in a good place.

The next part of this book includes my own stories, which are meant to provide examples of how we can function in a new age. Everything I understood about Christianity came tumbling down. What I experienced in the heavenly realms didn't match what I'd been taught, but I knew in my gut that what I experienced was right. How did I know that? It was bathed in love and demonstrated Yahweh's character and kindness. I didn't understand what was happening at first, but I innately knew to keep pushing forward. What solidified the whole process? I started seeing changes from the inside out. People started noticing those changes. I behaved differently. What used to cause negative triggers no longer had the same effect. The biggest change? Love was—and is—becoming my barometer, my plumb line.

In each of the following chapters, I share the heavenly encounter first. I do this so you can engage with each experience from your own perspective. Anything I introduce could influence your thinking process. Allow Yahweh to speak to you through my words. Allow your heart to be filled with Yahweh's love and truth as you enter the story. What does he say to you in this? Do you relate to anything I share? What else do you take from each story? Journal your thoughts as you read my encounters.

After I share each encounter, I explain what I learned and how the circumstances of that experience propelled me into my personal great awakening. Anything new we learn has the potential to propel us into a new season. In this case, it's a new age. New ages look vastly different from current ages. Each encounter taught me more about my responsibility in the Age of Aquarius. I didn't realize that purpose until I was given the mandate to write this book. Keep in mind the underlying message of each encounter; the Trinity showed me how heaven functions and what my role was in that process.

Finally, at the end of each chapter, I include an activation for you to practice. Practice takes patience and perseverance, so prepare to do something daily. My goal is to provide materials that help you on your own journey into the Age of Aquarius.

Take a deep breath. See yourself with Yeshua in a peaceful place. Allow your sanctified imagination to take you on a journey, a journey into the unknown of creation. Yeshua takes your hand and gently leads you in.

CHAPTER 7

SPEAKING TO THE STARS

I STAND WITH FATHER, Yeshua, and Holy Spirit in the middle of a dancing mist. As I follow the dance, a tunnel suddenly opens before me from the middle of the mist. Stars twinkle before me, and I sense it's okay to step in. Yeshua acknowledges my thoughts and grabs my hand. Into the tunnel we go.

For a moment, we watch what looks like slow moving lights that resemble stars. They seem to be circling around and around us. I'm reminded of how all creation is waiting for the Sons of Yahweh to get our act together so what's corrupt in creation can be restored to its original state.

The star's lights begin to move closer and closer to us. Yeshua turns in the opposite direction, opening his mouth. A mist-like substance flows out and integrates with the stars. They don't act any differently as they continue on a circular path.

"It's your turn," Yeshua instructs.

I open my mouth, not knowing what will come out. Nothing comes out, but then I realize that I'm holding my breath, so I start to breathe again. At that point, the same mist comes from me. I continue to hold my mouth open and breathe while watching the mist come up from within me. I know Yeshua is in me and I'm in him, so my assumption is that I'm releasing a piece of him that's in me.

"Sort of," Yeshua replies. "What's within you is unique to you. Yes, I'm in you, but the combination of what the two of us put together creates its own DNA breath print. These stars need that for this time. Now, sing!"

The song "Deep Waters" is playing, so I hum the B-flat. The sound intermingles with the mist. I realize it's a three-stranded cord: my breath, Yeshua's breath, and the song.[21]

For several hours, we stay in this position. One by one, the stars come up and ask for this fresh breath and song. I sing based on what music is playing in my house. When the song changes, my song changes. After some time, we step back to watch how the stars respond. I ponder the purpose for this.

"Remember, it requires the Sons of Yahweh to bring everything back into alignment." Yeshua answers my thoughts. "The beginning and the end all must be aligned so there truly is no beginning and end. They meet to create a continual flow."

"Can I know what we've done here, and what it affects?" I ask.

"What is the purpose of a star?" Yeshua questions.

"I don't really know," I respond. "My science background is a bit shallow."

Yeshua chuckles as he continues. "At least you're honest with that assessment. But what you would have learned in science classes is only part of the picture. Scientists are still discovering much about the stars. They aren't waste and are in the heavens for a purpose, mainly as frequency carriers. That is, they carry the frequency of the kingdom to the outermost limits of the universe so that, as new dimensions are created, the forming process starts with the proper frequency. As of now, so much is still in chaos."

Yeshua stops for a moment, looking at me intently. I know he's about to say something very important. "The musicians—my musicians—are so important. They must release the frequencies from within them. I've put those frequencies there. That's why you continued this process of breathing and singing to the stars in your sleep. Your spirit was at attention while your music continued to play all through the night. Every musician has a sound to release that affects the cosmos."

"So when those frequencies are released, does it also allow the stars to emanate that frequency into the atmosphere?" I ask.

"That's part of it," another voice speaks.

I turn as Father joins our conversation. The three of us now stand together watching the stars. They've all slightly changed their direction to a harmonious complement of varying motions.

"That's the other part," Father continues. "The combined emanation from each star helps set creation in order—"

Yeshua interrupts. "It's a layered effect. It must be done in the heavens first to manifest on the earth."

We turn and continue to watch as the stars strike out on new paths, change colors, and learn how, when, and where to move.

What did I learn from this story?

Here is the big takeaway. I was in the beginning stages of understanding that I'm responsible for the entire cosmos as a Son of Yahweh. My actions and reactions affect all of creation. Until this point, my effect was limited to those in my sphere of influence. It didn't cross my mind that my actions could affect someone on the other side of the world, much less stars in the heavens. In this new move of Yahweh, many have taught that our DNA is an important key to our function. We're part of the creation process. That came through Yeshua because he joined with human DNA. As we understand who we are in Christ, many doors we never knew existed open.

What I share in this chapter often creates major paradigm shifts for people. Until we understand our authority as Sons of Yahweh, we'll struggle to walk in these truths. When we suffer from self-esteem issues, rejection, an attitude that we're not good enough, or a myriad of other situations, functioning out of our identity becomes a bit tricky. My first book, *Accessing the Kingdom Realms*, was my experience about understanding identity. Just like everything else, it takes practice to change mindsets.

How did this story help with my personal great awakening?

To walk through an awakening experience, we must first understand that we're created to function as spirit beings. We have a body, soul, and spirit. They are supposed to work together. Just like the temple needed an outer court, inner court, and the holy of holies, we need our three-part being. Why? We are the temple of the Holy Spirit. From that position of being in Christ, we resonate what comes from within our holy of holies (our spirit) to everything outside of us. This is the most intimate place with the Trinity. We are to learn to function from this position twenty-four hours per day, seven days a week. That takes time and practice.

World circumstances can dictate our responses. An awakening requires that we look to the heart of Yahweh rather than news, social media, friends, family, or other sources for our daily bread. We don't put blinders on to ignore the circumstances. Our goal is to keep our focus on Christ during the chaos around us. That's why 1 Thessalonians 5:18 tells us to give thanks *in* everything, not *for* everything. We get what we need by communing with Yahweh from that intimate place *in* him. As I understand how the parts of the temple work in me, I'm learning to grasp and tap into the true flow of Yahweh's love.

Activation!

Pull up a picture of Solomon's temple. Inside the temple grounds, several places allowed people to move about, depending on their level of authority as a Jew. Any Jew could enter the outer court. The inner court, holy place, and holy of holies have progressively strict rules about who can enter. I relate the inner court to the physical body, the holy place to the soul, and the holy of holies to the spirit. Most often, we function from the body, letting it dictate many of our responses. But we should instead function from the spirit first. Then, we should allow that to flow into the soul and, finally, to the body. This is functioning from a place of pure intimacy with Yahweh—our place of worship.

Take some time to marinate in the holy of holies. Say or sing the names of Yahweh the way the priests used to. Then, imagine those frequencies intermingling with the blood on the altar—the blood of Yeshua. Together, they resonate to create an energy that brings life. Release love to YHVH and receive his love for you. Allow love to infuse you to the very core of your being. Let love become a part of you. Nothing else matters but the love of Yahweh.

Next, watch as that love moves from your spirit into your soul, the holy place. In this place, you may be prompted to deal with some soul issues. Remember that love covers all. There's no reason to think poorly of yourself should something come up that you may be embarrassed about. See how love transforms you. I suggest that you do this often but don't try to deal with more than one issue at a time. Let the Holy Spirit direct you. At times, you won't sense anything needs to be done. Awesome! Simply continue releasing Yahweh's love into your soul.

Finally, see Yahweh's love flow into your body, the outer court. Release love into every part of your physical body that needs a bit of tender loving care. Imagine your entire being as a whole entity that functions from the inside out—spirit first, soul second, and body third. From this position—from that intimate place with Father—we reign over our lives.

CHAPTER 8

EXPANSIVENESS OF CREATION

Yeshua grabs my hand and almost instantly, everything around us seems to look like a wispy starry night but with plenty of light. We zoom upward, higher and higher until only the expansiveness of the cosmos is visible. Earth looks like a speck of dust from this position. As I look back toward the earth, a distinct humming seems to vibrate through this entire place. I wonder where we are and where we're going.

"You need to see the expansiveness of creation." Yeshua answers my thoughts. "As you understand how this was all done, you'll have answers to the why question in all of this."

I quietly look around, gazing at the wonder of this starry universe that surrounds us.

"Where are we?" I ask.

"The beginning," Yeshua answers quickly. "We're in a different dimension where one dimension leads to another. They are all connected."

I look around at what seems like an empty space with glowing stars. The hum is still evident, an underlying fundamental frequency. Yeshua tells me it's the voice of Yahweh. Gazing in every direction, I look for the source of the sound.

"Creation itself is the voice of Yahweh," Yeshua says, answering my thoughts. "You hear it as one sound even though it's a symphony of sounds. It's all harmonious because it comes from the same source with a specific intent during the creation process. One sound may go this way and another sound that way to create two different things. Ultimately, they create a full symphony of complimentary frequencies. That's why shapes, colors, musical notes, things in nature, and mathematics all complement each other. They become intertwined in a creative process."

I ponder this a moment as I continue to listen to the humming. It permeates the whole atmosphere. But nothing appears to respond to it, which seems odd.

"That's because it still needs the intent of Yahweh to organize the sounds to do what they're supposed to do. Each has a purpose, and that purpose hasn't been assigned at this point. Remember, we're at the beginning of time."

For a moment, I focus on the hum.

"Move your arms," instructs Yeshua.

I take this to mean conduct, so I begin to conduct the symphony in different time signatures. I ponder on all the great composers who created a sense of motion through varying tempo changes. After some time, there is faint motion, and ever so quietly, a rhythmic beat starts. The humming begins to respond.

"You see," Yeshua states, "there is even intent in motion. Creation responds to you because of your sonship. You have DNA, and creation responds to that sound."

"How does that work through motion?" I ask.

"Motion organizes frequencies. Rhythm is not only sound but motion. This is one way to bring chaos into order. Rhythmically saying and repeating things solidifies a thing. Everything works together in this creative process. You see it in music: rhythm, melody, and harmony. The entire universe responds to those three things."

For a moment, I simply ponder. Besides paralleling the three-stranded cord, it parallels intent, desire, and action or thoughts, intents, and action. They are all benches of three—three things needed to make a whole. As a group of three, they create a governmental authority over a thing. Creation appears to need at least three key ingredients for a recipe.

"Everything starts with a thought, as you describe so well in your articles. That's part of what holding people in your heart means. You hold them there and release our intent over them. Notice that when you conducted, movement, a positioning, occurred. With positioning, the next step can begin. At times, movement can even be intent by itself. Remember that intent has a frequency."

I continue to listen to the hum as I ponder Yeshua's words. It's constant—the continual voice of Yahweh—as described by the observer in quantum physics.

Yeshua turns his head to the left and breathes. Out comes three streams of color that appear to dance with the particles in the cosmos. Somehow, I sense these are the voices in three parts of Father, Son, and Holy Spirit. The moment this thought flits through my mind, Father and Holy Spirit appear. They meld into one being, the three colors remaining constant and continuous.

With a twinkle in Father's eye, he says, "That surprised you, didn't it?"

"Nothing seems to surprise me anymore," I respond, giggling.

This only makes sense because Yeshua was with Father at the beginning. He saw everything. When Father breathed, Yeshua breathed with him. I knew this in my head, but now, I feel it in my heart.

"Yes, you understand," Father replies. "And you saw only Yeshua at first, but as you watched, we are truly all one. Are you ready for more?"

I turn back toward the three strands of light of colors. They appear to emanate all the colors of the rainbow, but they're never the same color at the same time. I then realize the humming sound is coming directly from Father, the Source. At the same time, it's everywhere. The entire universe resonates with his sound. His very act of being creates this resonance.

"It's the fundamental frequency. All others come out of that, just as you've learned through the musical harmonic series. There's always a main pitch and all other pitches are by-products of the original note. There's always a main frequency, the base. What's released from that base, the other frequencies then respond according to their proper harmonics. They are all harmonious with the base or fundamental frequency. Therefore, you see both the sound and reaction."

I take a moment to ponder this. Yes, I understand it, but Father's explanation sheds new light on how it all works together.

He continues, "This is why you see the source along with a reaction. Some places have been corrupted because of the fall. As a son, this is where you step in to right the fundamental frequency. This is partially what your music does. The introduction of the fundamental tone releases the tones above and below it that then resonate with and complement it. Your intent becomes infused with the fundamental frequency. When that intent is laced with my love, it overrides what occurred at the fall. It's a restoration process. At times, you're not even aware of it. Be obedient to open your mouth or play an instrument or release a sound when you feel led to do so. That's where it all starts."

What did I learn from this story?

First, I had no idea at the beginning of my come-up-here journey that I was ultimately responsible for the care of all of creation. I have my part and so does everyone else. This story is an example of doing what I saw my Father do. Then, I followed his lead. I had many opportunities to practice.

Everything begins with a thought. This is extremely important. I learned to understand at a deeper level how this process worked, from the very first thought Yahweh had, which included mankind. All Yahweh wants is relationship with creation, which is built into the fabric of the cosmos where everything functions together in harmony.

How did this story help with my personal great awakening?

If we don't understand that we're part of the creative process, we can't awaken to our position as Sons of Yahweh. We must first understand our identity from the position of a son, much like the prodigal son. Once the son understood his true identity, he could step into it. Until then, he wandered around. For years, I floundered because I didn't understand the fullness of my authority in Christ. I discovered that I didn't need a pastor, apostle, prophet, or teacher to take me to the Source. I'm learning that I can go to heaven now and not wait until I die.

A great awakening occurs when we get outside ourselves and realize that we're part of a much bigger picture—the entire cosmos. When we learn that we are priests and kings, we have the freedom to make big decisions, function with great authority, and step into our role with maturity. We're learning to answer the groaning of creation.

This encounter also showed me that even motion is part of the creative process. When we make motions, intent is involved, both conscious and unconscious.

Activation!

Position yourself in a place or worship. If it helps, put on some music. Begin to worship Yahweh by speaking or singing in tongues. Focus your intention on the purpose of worship.

If you don't yet speak in tongues, invite Yahweh to show you what you need to do. If the concept doesn't make sense to you, I recommend that you get a book by Kenneth Hagin titled, *Why Tongues?*[22]

Spend some time worshiping in tongues. You may sense, see, hear, or feel things as you do this. Move, draw, paint, dance, or do whatever you feel led to do. After some time, allow the scenery around you to change where the ceiling of possibility opens before you. Ask any member of the Trinity (or all of them) to show you more of the expansiveness of creation. Allow them to take you on an adventure.

You may understand none of what you see, but that's okay. Go with it and simply allow Yahweh to give you a tour of creation. Allow your adventure to be anywhere within creation. Be sure to journal your experiences. The more you do this exercise, the more you'll understand what you see. As you write down each experience, understanding will increase.

CHAPTER 9

A CABIN IN THE WOODS

I begin to worship, seeing myself in the heavenly realms. I'm in a large grassy field with arms outstretched, worshiping with all my might while a mist swirls around me. The blades of grass beneath my feet begin to sway with my movements. Soon enough, the mist fades, revealing a beautiful countryside. Off in the distance is a log cabin set back among some trees. Excited, I run full speed toward the cabin.

As I approach the cabin, potted plants are at the bottom of the stairs. On the deck are lawn chairs, a couple of tables, and many more potted plants. For me, this is a dream home, but I walk past all of it, heading straight for the front door. I'm compelled to enter through a heavily decorated wooden door with scenes of events. I can tell that the carvings tell a story but for now, I move onward. I bust through the door. Father, Yeshua, and Holy Spirit are all sitting around a massive stone fireplace that envelops an entire wall from floor to ceiling. An enormous fire sparkles and crackles in an oversized firebox opening.

Father sits comfortably in an easy chair that faces the fireplace. Tonight, he's dressed in his logger outfit, which tells me this is a comfortable and personal work meeting, not about business. To the right, Yeshua is sitting on a sofa that faces the center of the room. He too is wearing work clothing. His beard reaches down his chest, and his arms stretch out across the back of the sofa with legs crossed. With a twinkle in his eye, he invites me to come sit with him. Directly across from him is Holy Spirit sitting on another sofa. His bright white clothing sets off the ocean-blue of his eyes that seem to constantly move. All three face the center of the room as they look into each other's eyes.

I join Yeshua and sit close enough that our beings touch. As I connect with him, I feel as if I'm melding into him. It's like an optical illusion where you're half in and half out of something.

For a moment, we sit quietly together as I take in the atmosphere. I open my mouth, and out comes a stream of colors. Father opens his mouth, and the colors from my mouth go into him. Holy Spirit opens his mouth, and out comes musical frequencies. They come towards me. I open my mouth again, and the frequencies slide right in. Yeshua opens his mouth, and out comes smells—cinnamon and other sweet spices. Somehow, I understand this to be communication, and the words are motion, color, sound, and smell. I have the feeling that we're viewing words at a microscopic level.

"Very observant!" Father says. "Everything out of your mouth is important. Now, you can see what words look like. Had they been words contrary to our character, what you saw would look much different."

Chiming in, Yeshua adds, "You're only seeing part of how that operates, how words create. Now, you might understand why the Hebrew language was pictographic at first."

"I get it now!" I respond excitedly.

"The creative force of words begins in the thought realm. Eventually, those thoughts are set into words. That's why you see even the same words come out as something different at times," Holy Spirit airily responds.

His voice sounds like a wind that then forms into words. I sit and take all this in. I look back as our conversation intermingles in shapes, colors, and waveforms. They do a little dance. Once they come into agreement, everything then turns into one specific thing—a frequency or dancing color. Occasionally, a whiff of some fragrance floats by.

"You see," Yeshua says, "all words create a frequency. The thoughts and intents often determine what that frequency looks like. That's why it's important to take thoughts captive so ugly images don't form."

As I continue to ponder, I look around the cabin. The logs are alive. I remember a discussion I had with a real estate agent about how log homes breathe, which requires a different type of care than a standard home.

Hearing my thoughts, Yeshua asks, "So what does that have to do with this?"

"Uh... everything is breathing and living?" I question.

"That's one level of it. But there's more," Yeshua adds. "The memory of everything each tree came into contact with from the seedling state is still in those logs. The only part that's missing is the bark, which was used to protect it. When a log is added to a home, it carries the memory of the entire area from which it came."

I reflect on the water videos and how water carries the record of everything put into it. I gather that would only make sense. As a tree soaks up any liquid, it will carry the record of what surrounds it when the tree drinks from the earth.

Answering my thoughts, Father says, "When something carries that memory, it holds it. Pristine trees harvested from a forest often become part of a log cabin. They are transferred to a new location where the memory of where they were raised is brought with them. That frequency then radiates to the area around it. Have you ever wondered why log homes seem to have similar décor, no matter what century it is or where they are found?"

"I'd not thought much about that." I answer honestly.

"The record of what's in those memory banks is delivered wherever that item goes. Yes, matter does have memory," Yeshua continues. "You have read stories about how transplant recipients suddenly have a change of preferences and tastes. That's because their new organs carry the memory of the person they came from. Not only that, but those organs also have a memory of everyone in their generational line as well!"

I ponder how this is important to what I'm working on now.

Holy Spirit breathes, and a mist begins to fill the cabin. Father and Yeshua close their eyes and allow this to resonate through them. Eventually, there is a buzzing, and objects in the room start to vibrate at a level of a hum that I can now hear. I look up. The log walls appear to receive this sound. In a sense, they hold a record of what's going on in the room, adding to the record of what was in the earth while they grew.

"Everything works together, connecting all the pieces, so it functions the way it was intended. This is where matter meets memory. Then, you take the memory and direct it to respond to the frequencies as set up from the beginning of time," Father instructs.

"So let me see if I get this right," I say, pausing to collect my thoughts. "We consider and understand that everything around us carries memory. It's up to us as Sons of Yahweh to release what's directly from you into what's around us. That means everything functions as intended from the beginning of time."

What did I learn from this story?

This encounter came as I researched how matter carries memory. Not long after I created the first music essence, I ran across some documentaries on water memory. I began blogging about them on the Healing Frequencies Music website. That information helped me understand how and why essences work. By the time this encounter occurred, I already had bits and pieces of the information. Here, the Trinity ties it all together for me. This encounter helped me connect some of the unknown and lingering dots. This was the biggest takeaway from the story; it connected puzzle pieces and solidified research. In addition, I learned how frequency works at a deeper level. This understanding is part of my mandate for the Age of Aquarius.

I really enjoyed spending this time with the Trinity in a log home. I adore log homes, and Yahweh spoke to me through a vision where I felt comfortable. Papa (Father) knows this, so many encounters I have with the Trinity occur in a log home, a place of intimacy. I always know the tone of these meetings based on how they're dressed. I have fond memories of my own father taking us into the woods to gather firewood, wearing his logging clothes. I have a strong relationship with my earthly father, so these settings bring me warm fuzzies. Father God often meets us in the places that are special to us.

How did this story help with my personal great awakening?

I began to understand more deeply the importance of even breath as part of the creative process. This is Yahweh's perspective on how matter carries memory. When we step into a renewal or an awakening, we need to dissect every part of our being. We see what works and what doesn't. We awaken to a need for adjustment in an area where we were previously clueless. Yahweh enables us to facilitate needed changes through activation, which garners greater understanding of what's on the scroll of our lives.

Activation!

If you could meet Yeshua anywhere, where would that be? Go to that place and invite him to join you. Sit close enough that you can feel his heartbeat resonating throughout your entire being. Take time to quiet your mind. Focus on seeing love flow through every vein in your body. Follow this trail in your imagination and watch what Yahweh's love does as it travels from your head all the way down to your toes. The key here is to allow your being to resonate with the love that's coming from within Yahweh.

Yahweh may show you things from your past that need some attention. Go with it, see what he shows you, and then journal about it. In the future, you can see how this ties to other areas, and you will see how much you've grown.

I encourage you to put on some peaceful instrumental music, such as any of the Healing Frequencies Music on the website.[23] Spotify, iTunes, YouTube, and various other streaming services carry this music. Allow yourself to stay in this position with Yeshua until you feel at rest. Journal what you sense, see, hear, and feel. You are learning to recognize pure love. As you do this from that secure position with Yeshua, see yourself in him. You're part of him and he's part of you. Release your love to him as you receive his love.

CHAPTER 10

JACOB AND HIS SPECKLED AND SPOTTED FLOCKS

After reading papers and watching documentaries of scientists researching water memory, one researcher casually mentioned Jacob and his use of water to produce spotted and speckled sheep. (See Genesis 30:25–43.) Intrigued by this idea, I desired to engage with Jacob and ask him about these Bible events.

I position myself in the kingdom of Yahweh with an intent to understand more of who Yahweh is and how he works. I excitedly wait. Colors soon start to float by me. I sense that I'm in the midst of what Jacob engaged with. The colors change form and shape as heavenly music comes from everywhere. These shapes seem as if they can become anything and are only waiting for intent to finalize the process. Am I in a place of creation? The clouds swirl and move to the music, not only in this place but in my home as well. This musical conversation occurs between two realms. Everything in this place interacts with one another. Bits and pieces of matter float around, and then suddenly, they connect and become a recognizable object: a shape, a figure, a musical composition, a piece of artwork, etc. Could Jacob have possibly come to this place to create the desired look for his flocks? Did he then put the revelation of that knowledge into the water the flocks drank from?

"You are correct." A voice booms behind me.

I immediately sense it's Jacob and turn. A man stands there, dressed in a long flowing robe in shepherd's attire that I'm used to seeing in pictures. His brown hair and beard flow over his tanned face. He looks a lot like Yeshua. At that thought, he smiles.

"You are in a place where things are formed from thoughts, intents, and desires," Jacob says as he approaches me.

"Thank you for meeting me here."

This is all that I can muster up. I'm actually quite shocked that I have the privilege of this meeting.

"You're welcome! Your desire has brought you here. And you've taken the time to search a matter out. Those together lead towards vision," he expresses.

"As I'm learning," I reply.

I turn. Yeshua has joined us. Standing next to Jacob, they look like twins, both around the age of thirty.

"Everything is created through thought first," Yeshua says, getting right to the point. "Then, the thoughts frame the intent. Intent leads to desire, which then creates matter. Here, in a place of creation, all the necessary ingredients sit, waiting for the Sons of Yahweh to create."

I look around. So much matter appears to be suspended in the air. It's against a white background, which tells me creative pieces are suspended in light itself.

"Exactly!" Yeshua exclaims.

"As you have heard before," Jacob adds, "We understood more than your generation how to ascend and create what was needed. It's in here—a kingdom laboratory where it begins. You read the Hebrew during your studies for the verses in Genesis 30 where you saw that I understood what to do to attain the desired result."

"I'm guessing you understood that water carries memory," I ponder.

"All the ancients understood that," he casually replies.

"Scientists are only beginning to understand so much about water," adds Yeshua. "You see, it's a life force in so many ways. Modern man has yet to grasp its fullness."

"I understood that what I create up here can be released through water," Jacob reveals. "You did that with the music essences for all of your albums. At first, you lacked understanding and did it by faith because Yeshua gave you instructions how to do it. The revelation of truth came later."

I ponder this for a moment, realizing he's absolutely accurate in that assessment. By the time I created the second music essence (the 713 Hertz), I understood more about water memory. The 528 Hertz essence came from an encounter with Yeshua when I was given specific instructions on what to do. This action of stepping out in faith led to more essence-making.[24] My ponderings lead to another question.

"Jacob, when you had the flocks face a certain direction, could they literally see the doorway to what you created in the kingdom realms?" I ask.

"That's exactly what I did," he answers. "Look at the word *ring-strake*. The Hebrew letters are *ayin, qof,* and *dalet*. This indicates that the fountain of time opened a door. Now look at verse thirty-nine."

I open the verse in Biblewheel.com where I can compare the Hebrew words with the English (KJV). Here are the words:

- conceived = *yod, chet,* and *mem*. Together, these letters mean the hand has the power to divide water
- before the rods = *mem,* qof, *lamed*. Water comes around in a circle of time toward (upon, into). The rods themselves refer to a germination process.
- and brought forth = *yod, lamed, dalet*. The hand with the power, the yoke looking through the door.
- flocks = *tsadik, aleph, final nun*. A harvest of the head of the seed (heir).

- ringstraked = ay*in, qof, dal*et. The fountain (eye) in the circle of time goes through that door.[25]

Jacob watches as I Google and then write down what I find. After I have a synopsis, he continues. "When you set your eyes before something, you look upon it and bring the revelation of what you see into desire. I desired and purposed for my flocks to look a certain way. Therefore, I created my desire in this kingdom laboratory. I then released it into the water that the flocks drank. But at the same time, their eyes were upon that desire. This combination created an arc, an energy that brought forth the desired result."

"The same thing happens with electricity," Yeshua adds. "You have a negative and a positive. They must function together to create the needed arc that then creates an electrical current. Electricity is energy. Energy creates."

I ponder all this while surveying the laboratory. No lab tables or other typical lab equipment is present. Chuckling at my thoughts, Yeshua comments, "In this place, creation starts with a thought. It's one of many similar labs. It won't look like what you're used to seeing on Earth. When you're creating a mindset, a paradigm, or even matter, you start with a thought. Even when something unhelpful is created, you make adjustments and start over just as you would with any experiment. So you must bring the intent of Yahweh to your recipe."

"If I come here creating things that shouldn't be created and I realize the error, what am I to do?" I ask.

"Put the pieces back and ask for the best recipe. This shows you are walking in a greater level of maturity. Do this from a pure heart and motive. That brings about the desired result. When you function in the center of the Name—Yod, Heh, Vav, Heh (YHVH)—I'm standing with you, and we are in the center together. It then becomes Yod, Heh, Shin, Vav, Heh (YHSVH) where we do it together. That brings about the best result."

I ponder this for a moment, not realizing that I can adjust as needed. I visualize how that might look. Yeshua interrupts my thoughts. "The key here is to function out of maturity. As you grow in that, you'll have a better idea how to assemble what you need in your desire. That knowledge comes from relationship with the Trinity."

Yeshua gives me a big hug. His love flows through me as I soak in his encouragement.

Jacob adds, "Yes, once you understand how to assemble the desires, you can more easily bring a needed action. This is true of any lab with ongoing experiments. Adjustments are made as needed to attain the desired result. Put back something if you realize it isn't necessary! It's new and usable for the future."

"You don't need to be impatient," Yeshua instructs. "Each Son of Yahweh has a timetable that works best for him or her. No two people are alike, so be sure to stay with us, the Trinity. We will help walk you through this process. You can come here and watch us create. 'Like father, like son.' This is how you learn: you watch, then you do."

What did I learn from this story?

It never crossed my mind that the Bible included examples of water memory. Of course, upon realizing this truth, I desired to engage with the story so I could see for myself. I'd practiced stepping into Bible stories, so this wasn't new to me. I went in with no expectations. I had an intense desire to examine how this worked from a heavenly perspective. I knew that I was missing something amazingly simple, and enquiring minds wanted to know.

I learned that even in encounters that seem rather odd, a biblical precedent is generally present somewhere. We may not recognize what that is because our mindsets tend to lead us to the mundane, the common, and the ordinary. This required stepping out of my comfort zone to see an old story with a new perspective. This encounter also helped me understand that we create from a heavenly perspective first, then release what we've created into the earth realm.

How did this story help with my personal great awakening?

All awakenings require a change in mindset. My willingness to see Scripture from a fresh perspective helped me understood the deeper mysteries of how things are created in heaven first. By the end of the encounter, random thoughts began to solidify, which in turn helped me understand more of Yahweh's character. As Sons of Yahweh, we're called to create. This story helped me understand the creative process of making music essences, which involved using water to carry memory. It's important to note that I'd already created one music (sound) essence by this point. But I did it at the direction of Yeshua without the knowledge of how and why they worked. Here, I was given the understanding.

Our thoughts, intents, and actions create a three-stranded cord that's not easily broken. Everything begins with a thought. Desire germinates intent from which action is born. Actions most often start with words. Life and death are in the power of the tongue. (See Proverbs 18:21.) We choose to create life or death with our thoughts, intents, and words.

Going deeper, I realized the importance of creating in heaven first and then releasing that reality into the earth. By faith, just like Jacob who put his flocks in a position to see their mandate, I had hope that when I do the same thing, I will see similar results.

Activation!

Write down several Scriptures that are particularly meaningful to you. Ponder what they mean from the perspective of a loving Yahweh who wants nothing but the best for his children. Next, step into a Scripture and see how Yahweh unpacks it. You may be prompted to look up meanings for various words as I was instructed to do in my encounter. Wait to see how Yahweh uses the experience for your benefit.

Let's use Psalm 91 as an example. I'll provide the first few verses to get you started. I copied and pasted the Scripture into a document, then changed the wording, so it was personal to me. Here is the original Scripture.

> Whoever dwells in the shelter of the Most High
> will rest in the shadow of the Almighty.
> I will say of the Lord, "He is my refuge and my fortress,
> my God, in whom I trust."
> Surely, he will save you
> from the fowler's snare
> and from the deadly pestilence.
> He will cover you with his feathers,
> and under his wings you will find refuge;
> his faithfulness will be your shield and rampart.

Here is a deeper personal version for your encounter:

> I dwell in the shelter of the Most High where I
> rest in the shadow of the Almighty.
> I will say of the Lord, "You are my refuge and
> my fortress,
> my God, in whom I trust."
> Surely you will save me
> from the fowler's snare
> and from the deadly pestilence.
> You will cover me with your feathers,
> and under your wings I will find refuge;
> your faithfulness will be my shield and rampart.

After completing your own personalization of the passage, step into a quiet place and visualize where this shelter might be. We're given a picture of being protected under wings. What does that look like to you? Go to that place and engage with how this protection feels. Read each verse slowly while seeing yourself in that place. Say out loud to the Lord that he is your refuge. Decree and declare that he saves you from the fowler's snare and any deadly pestilence.

Speak directly to any circumstance or disease so that it comes into alignment with this Scripture.

Take time to stay under the wings. What sense do you have while you're there? How does Yahweh's faithfulness feel like a shield and a rampart? See yourself freed from anything that plagues you. Then continue through the rest of Psalm 91, allowing the Lord to speak to you about each verse. Each engagement leads to another level of revelation. Do this until you feel you have a release to move onto another Scripture.

As you do similar activations with other Bible verses, this will increase your courage because you're using Scripture as an ascension platform.

CHAPTER 11

Repentance in the Court

An angel ushers me to an observation area of a court session in process. Angels appear before the judge, bringing stacks of papers. A bit of chaos ensues as more piles of documents are brought into the court. Eventually, individuals scuffle on the witness stand, and something is hauled off. But I can't hear anything, as if I'm watching a silent movie.

Chief Tall Feather, my city's angel, stands before the court. Other angels then step forward with additional paperwork. While the court session continues, I am back in my heart garden under the Camperdown Elm tree. Papa (Father) is with me. I call him "Papa" because it helps me feel closer to him. He also allows me to call him this.

"Papa, what is going on here, and why am I not able to hear?"

"Some things are much bigger than you realize at this point. As you pointed out, the Federal Highway Administration is involved in this lawsuit that came from the environmental group toward the state. This is now a national issue. The Ninth Circuit Court has the case. You're right, certain laws for your state play a part. However, so much more is involved," Papa answers.

As I ponder what's taking place in the court, I then walk along a carefully manicured row of hedges. It's as if I'm flipping from scene to scene where I have an important part to play. I've walked by this hedge before and recognize Father's garden. As I think this, Papa joins me. Then, Yeshua and Holy Spirit appear. We walk in silence together for quite some time. I focus on staying in step with their movements and walking speed. I sense this is a time to be in the center of YHVH. I continue to ponder on the courtroom situation and the process of being displaced by a highway project.

"Trials are part of what forms and tests you. This whole situation with the highway displacement is testing and building your character. How that works is up to you," Papa speaks casually, yet with resolve.

I know this is my cue to repent for some bad attitudes.

"You know what to do with that," Yeshua adds.

"Yes, I believe that I do," I answer. "I own a rotten attitude, hatefulness, disdain, cruelty, bitterness, and resentment towards the Idaho Transportation Department and the environmental group that's suing them."

Although I know that I am not personally guilty of every attitude, I sense that I'm repenting on behalf of my entire neighborhood as well. I've heard the words but didn't deal with them at that time. In a sense, I've agreed with what was spoken because of my own frustrations. Therefore, I own and repent for all that comes to mind. It renders the enemy powerless, which I take great excitement in doing.

"Now, do you understand why you couldn't hear what was going on in the court session?" Papa asks.

"My issues kept me from hearing," I plainly state.

"As you know well, wrong attitudes block your ability to participate. When you are quick to take care of anything contrary to my character, you will be open to receiving greater authority. Now that you've dealt with it, would you like to go back and hear what you missed?" Papa asks with a smile.

"Yes!" I exclaim.

The next thing I know, I'm right back in the court room where I first saw Chief Tall Feather. I'm still in the observation area with many in the cloud of witnesses. Elijah, Moses, and King David are with me. Moses is on one side of me while King David and Elijah are on the other side. As I look again, I have more clarity in my vision.

I'm being called to the bench.

Father says, "You have just repented of several sins. Do likewise for the entire case on behalf of those within the Idaho Transportation Department (ITD) and the environmental group."

Standing in front of the bench, I repent for these two groups as well as the Federal Highway Administration. As I end the repentance process, individuals scuffle in the witness box.

"Where would you like these to go?" Yeshua asks.

"To the abyss," I reply without even thinking.

They are taken away, hissing and screaming. They are those thoughts, attitudes, and actions that hindered me, including my vision and understanding of Yahweh's plan for this project.

The scene in the courtroom changes as we move from one court to another.

What did I learn from this story?

As the story indicates, I'm in the process of losing my home to a highway project. When our neighborhood found out about the project in the summer of 2012, we were heartbroken. But everything was not settled concerning the relocations until the summer of 2019. In those seven years, I had a lot to learn. First off, the relocation wasn't about me at all. Yes, it involved me, but the picture was much bigger than I imagined.

Traditional understanding is that we go before Yahweh, praying for those being displaced. Or we pray the project doesn't happen. After all, no one wants to lose a home to a highway project. We ask the big questions, "What's going to happen to me? Where am I going?

What will I do?" I admit that I was no different. However, shortly after the Draft Environmental Impact Statement came out in the spring of 2013, I attended a hearing on the project, agreeing openly with the state's decision. I downloaded the entire document (more than one thousand pages) and read it from cover to cover. The page that discussed our neighborhood included a picture of a bridge that was scheduled to be built over our homes. That picture mirrored a prophetic word I'd received in 2010 about how my life would look. I immediately thought twice about the project as it pertained to my own selfish interests.

During this seven-year process of uncertainty, I learned to function from a position of creativity amid chaos. Three of my four books came out during these seven years. I recorded the first eleven albums of my music, started a new business, and sold an old business. Everything in my life completely rearranged itself. Everything I thought I knew and understood about life's challenges crumbled. Yahweh used this situation to show me his will concerning the highway. Simultaneously, I stepped into a new understanding of his character and my role in this project. I share more of that process in the next story.

How did this story help with my personal great awakening?

The biggest effort in any awakening is to shift our thinking from what we've been taught to what Yahweh shows us. This new age is based on personal revelation that comes directly from the heart of Yahweh. Without practical application, teachings have little if any effect on our lives. When we engage with heaven, we partner with the creation process, which directly impacts how we function in Earth.

My personal great awakening involved stepping into the kingdom realms and developing a personal relationship with Yahweh *in* heaven. Yahweh is as close as the air we breathe. We only need to step in and engage. I can participate in all that heaven has now while I'm fully alive. When I understood this concept, everything changed for me. It was truly a great awakening! Repentance is a key in the process as well.

Activation!

The focus of this encounter was to bring me to a place where I was mature enough and could not only see but hear everything that was presented. A functional parent assists a child in the learning process. Father God is no different. Yahweh is gentle and kind in walking us through each circumstance. I understood from my previous experiences that this was a different court from the mobile court, which I discuss in my previous book.

Get into a quiet place where you can focus on Father, Son, and Holy Spirit. See yourself in that peaceful place with them. Picture a pool of water that's surrounded by a beautiful forest. Get into the water and take a bath in the love and glory of Yahweh, cleansing anything that needs washing. See it permeate every cell of your body. Past circumstances in your life may come to mind. Ask Yahweh to show you what your attitude was during those times. If you were not walking in love, go through a simple repentance. Sometimes I have a visual image to focus on, and other times, I do the entire action by faith without sensing, seeing, or hearing anything. In fact, it took months of doing this activation before I saw anything.

I use this quick activation in the process of opening my spiritual eyes *and* ears when an attitude keeps me from participating in what Yahweh has for me. I follow this process:

1. Own the attitude or behavior. I often say something like "I own fear."
2. Begin the repentance process by saying something like "I renounce all ties to fear and repent on behalf of myself and my entire generational line all the way back to Adam." NOTE: I do this whether I feel like it or not. I'm not led by feelings because, sometimes, the issue relates more to what others hold over me. When someone says that I operated out of fear,

I repent for that anyway because the words dangle before me, waiting to land. Someone aimed those words at me in accusation. Therefore, I take care of it so the words no longer sit staring at me, waiting for me to engage with them.

3. I then take fear to the cross and say, "I nail fear to the cross where it is crucified."

4. I then say, "I take fear through the cross and allow the blood of Yeshua to cover it."

5. Now, I replace fear and trade it for the opposite spirit to fill the void. As an example, I trade fear for Yahweh's peace. If nothing specific comes to mind, I generally ask for more of Yahweh's love.

NOTE: If you don't see or hear anything or feel any warm fuzzies after repenting and completing these five steps, don't be concerned. Our feelings have nothing to do with this because it's a step of faith. As you continue to go through these steps, you will know the process is working when what used to trigger you no long has the same effect over you.

CHAPTER 12

THE HIGHER COURTS OF HEAVEN

After repenting for a bad attitude, I'm back in the observation area with Moses, Elijah, and David. They have helped me so much on my journey of sonship. Here, they cheer me on to victory. Since I have dealt with the junk in myself, my ability to hear this heavenly court proceeding has been opened. My repentance opens the door for me to fully participate in this court session. I have no idea which court this is, nor does it matter.

More paperwork is collected, including the appeal from the environmental group. A bald man wearing a lawyer-like suit collects everything that's being brought into the court. The recent letter I'd written to the manager of the highway project appears at the top of the pile. The man hands the pile to Father, who places his hands on it before it disappears into him. A copy is left on the table. An angel then takes it away.

During this part of the session, Chief Tall Feather comes before the court.

"What do you have to present?" Father asks him.

"The petitions of the Sons of Yahweh and the righteous people of the land," he responds.

At this point, Chief Tall Feather hands Father a stack of prayers, many dating back to the time settlers first came to farm the land.

"I've worked with these people, even the Nez Perce and other tribes that used this land. This area is meant to be a place to gather and pass through, so it must continue to be safe for that purpose," he adds. He lays down another stack of papers. "I also present the Record of Decision by the Federal Highway Administration for this new highway. Let it be entered into the records."

An angel takes the paperwork from Chief Tall Feather and brings it to the bench where Father once again lays his hands on top of the pile. The information literally soaks into him before he sends an exact copy of it off to be recorded.

Upon completion of this set of paperwork, Chief Tall Feather steps aside, and a larger angel walks in. I now recognize him as the regional angel that watches over the northern section of Idaho along the Montana border. He turns and smiles at me as he approaches the bench.

"What have you brought before me today?" Father asks.

"The scroll for the region." The Chief's voice booms through the court. "This scroll shows and confirms what Chief Tall Feather has presented to you as well. The entire Hoo Doo mountain range is a pass through from south to north. Highway 95 currently follows it and is meant to be a carrier of holiness. As the highway is completed and updated from time to time, what's done in the natural by the Sons of Yahweh is a mirror of the supernatural."

He pauses for a moment as a court scribe writes his exact words. He then continues. "The Hoo Doos were overtaken by the enemy. This new highway, along with the revised highway further north, reflect what your sons are doing. I put my stamp of approval on the Highway Administration's Record of Decision as well as the work your sons are doing on the land."

The Chief then hands another stack of papers to Father. Some of them involve the rerouting of the highway around the Silverwood Theme Park as well as the recent improvements along various stretches of Highway 95. I focus on clearing out the junk on the land and opening this route for further travel. How that's to be done, I'm not sure.

Once again, Father places his hands over the pile, and it disappears into him but not without leaving an exact copy for an angel to take to a room where all the records are held. The Chief steps back and turns to me.

"This is your cue," Elijah says, whispering in my ear.

As he says this, the Chief motions for me to step forward. I walk toward the bench. Another angel is standing up front with him now that I don't know yet. He's also Native American and even larger than the Chief. I position myself between the two angels. We turn and face the bench.

Father says, "You now understand why you couldn't hear at first. Repentance puts you in a position to receive what I have for you, even when you're repenting on behalf of others."

"I understand that better now," I humbly say.

"You have papers for me too," he says, getting right to the point.

I look around for the papers before realizing they're in my heart. I pull them out. They include all my research for this project and the prayers of the intercessory team I worked with for over twenty years. Surprisingly, all the notes I'd taken at various conferences in the area are in the pile as well. Anything I've done that pertains to the call upon the northern panhandle of Idaho is with this paperwork. I've prepared for this moment for years and now realize this highway project is only a small part of the bigger picture.

"This is much bigger than you realize," Father answers my thoughts.

"I see that. And thank you for the reminder," I reply.

I quickly gather all the paperwork and hand an exceptionally large stack to Father. Again, he puts his hand on the pile. Everything soaks into him, but at the same time, it's left on the table. Maybe it's not an exact copy. Maybe he simply soaks up all the information into him and leaves the original pile for the angels to take away.

Turning his attention back to me, Father says, "As you see, angels assist you. You have Chief Tall Feather, the Chief, and this third angel. He's on the western side of Idaho that borders Washington."

The angel turns toward me. He has warrior gear with a full head-dress. He greets me with a handshake. "My name is Chief Mighty Warrior. I, too, am assigned to this region."

Father looks at the three of us, smiling.

"You now have three angels to work with you through the rest of your relocation process," Father instructs. "Now, release them to do what's needed on the land."

I turn as Chief Tall Feather returns to the front and stands with us.

"Release them to do their work," Father repeats.

I address each of them individually, releasing them to continue the journey we started together.

What did I learn from this story?

This highway project had little to do with my personal relocation. I had to take some time to rein in my emotions so that I wasn't functioning from a place of sorrow or grief over the loss of my home. Yahweh then began to show me snippets of my personal future, and I realized that everything would be fine. I became a spokesperson for the Idaho Transportation Department. They could not understand why someone losing their home would side with them. This step also shut up the voices in the environmental group who opposed the project. They had no desire to fight with me.

When I decided to partner with Yahweh in this transition, I was propelled into greater levels of authority as I also took care of my personal issues. I began to see how events twenty years earlier prepared me for this time. Our intercessory prayer team functioned in the supernatural and had years of notes that I saved. I eventually typed them all up and put them in a chronological order. As I incorporated what I learned in those prayer sessions through an ascended lifestyle, I began to powerfully operate in the courts.

My thoughts aren't always Yahweh's thoughts. What I think is important is often the opposite of the truth. My limited vision concerning this highway kept me in a box until saw the bigger picture. Once I realized that a prophetic word was coming to life, I looked deeper into the role of the highway and its purpose on the land.

How did this story help with my personal great awakening?

I was awakened to a deeper knowledge of Yahweh's character. Who I am, where I live, and what I do is only one piece of the puzzle. This thought process released me from a religious box so that I began to see situations through the eyes of the Trinity. My great awakening included functioning as part of this bigger picture. I no longer waited on Yahweh to do for me. As I stayed in a place of peace and rest *in* Christ, I became an active participant in the process. When I stepped away from my restful position, I learned to return to a place of repentance. Fear or anxiety desired to sit on my shoulders, hoping I'd let them in the door. Repentance kept me from taking the bait.

The current world circumstances are similar because we only see a small piece of what's really happening. The experience of my relocation helped me see and understand that Yahweh works in mysterious ways that are often very contrary to human thinking. I no longer push to make things happen. When I don't understand what's going on, I look through Yahweh's eyes and seek his heart on a matter.

Activation!

Make a list of current circumstances in your life with the most important issues at the top of the list. Take an item on the list and put it in your heart. Prophetically write out the act and place it over your heart. Write it in your journal as well. Then, leave space to write below. Remember, it took seven years for a circumstance I had no control over to be resolved. If it's a larger issue, the resolution may take time. You'll have many encounters about the same situation as you look for deeper understanding into what Yahweh is saying to you in and through it.

Be honest with yourself. As you write about the circumstance, be mindful of stinking thinking that may hamper progress. If something comes up, follow through with the repentance process until you're at rest and peace. To practice, you may want to start with smaller issues first.

Present the issue to Yahweh from a place of rest. I often see myself on a bench next to the River of Life under a Camperdown Elm tree. I talk about this tree in *Accessing the Kingdom Realms*. Here, I meet with Yeshua, Papa, and others in the cloud of witnesses. We talk and converse about various situations going on around me. As you visualize, find your own peaceful place where you're at rest and can meet with the Trinity.

Present the circumstance. Then, wait to see what occurs from that point forward. Don't be too quick to judge what you see, sense, hear, or feel. If you're new to this, you may only get snippets of information at a time. Practice, practice, practice. The more you engage with the Trinity at this level, the more you'll notice because your spiritual eyes (the eyes of your heart) are working more efficiently. As you continue, you'll be led to a greater level of understanding. Expect the unexpected. When something weird that you'd never even considered crosses through your mind, don't immediately reject it. Write it down and be sure to ask what it means.

CHAPTER 13

BUILDING A HIGHWAY

I stand in Him with a greater understanding that I can ask anything in his Name. As I see myself step into my position in Christ, I know that I have the authority to decree over my own relocation. This is the next step in the process of speaking over my new home.

I am hovering over the entire area where the highway will be built. I gaze down over the six-mile stretch as the highway materializes below me. A gentle wind blows me along the way—north and south along the entire route. I then stop above my own home and all of Benson's Mobile Home Park. The wind stops as I look down. I then sense it's time to make a decree.

"It's time," Yeshua says.

Taking a big breath, I blow over the entire neighborhood. Frequencies of color swirl out of my mouth. Then, the words flow. "May the highway be built as the ITD determines. I declare that the judge rules on behalf of the ITD and that this project will begin with no more delays. May those of us who must move be more than fairly compensated. Our new homes await us. They will be a total joy for us. May we be at peace during the entire process. I decree that ITD and the negotiators understand our needs and desires. Those needs will be met or exceeded. I say call forth those who are to assist with the relocation process for me and my neighbors. I decree that there will be no more delays!"

After the words come out of my mouth, a whirlwind of activity swirls, almost like a huge windstorm. It feels as if I'm moving ahead on the timeline.

A bulldozer comes to my yard, and with one giant claw, my house is down. I blink, wondering where I am on this timeline. The whirlwind starts again, and I go back a little further on the timeline. A moving van from City North American is parked outside my house, loading up. Both door sheds are on a flatbed trailer, ready to follow the moving van. The neighbors across the street are getting ready as well. I know that I'll be moving before they do.

Once again, the windstorm appears. We move forward in time. All the houses in the right-of-way zone are now gone. The first set of giant earth movers arrives to start the bridge. Several environmentalists who opposed the project are lying on the road to stop the bulldozers. The drivers patiently wait. They seem to know this was coming. Then, a Latah County Sheriff pulls up to take the protestors away.

As I continue to view various points on the timeline, I sense that I'm to breathe on the land. As I begin, a gentle breeze blows from the north to the south. The bridge over Eid Road is complete. The culverts are in, and huge amounts of soil are being removed from the top of Reisenauer Hill and then poured over the area where we used to live, filling it in with sixty feet of dirt. I again breathe on the land and earth movers. Then, I turn my focus to the areas on either side of the highway, knowing the environmentalists are concerned about this. I speak peace to the land. Grass seeds are sown into the land on either side of the highway as the completed highway materializes before my eyes.

Looking north, I continue along the same route, hovering above the highway where workers and big equipment continue to build the road toward town. As the process begins to wind down, I again speak peace over the land. I hover over the highway from the top of Reisenauer Hill and move toward the city, continually speaking peace over the land until I reach the section of the new highway that connects to the original highway.

In the blink of an eye, I'm again hovering above the whole highway, seeing it complete. Vehicles are now driving north and south. I come to a stopping point, and a large angel is standing next to me. Smiling, he wraps his arm around me. Somehow, I sense it's Chief Tall Feather.

He reminds me, "I was put in place many years ago by the Nez Perce tribe even though they weren't aware they'd done it. This land was a gathering place where many tribes came to collect camas root. You already know that part. More importantly, within this region, a fostering and caring spirit came with the native tribes who traveled here. That's the region's mandate."

"Thank you for what you've done," I say as I hug him. I ponder his words for a moment while we watch the cars travel up and down the highway. "May I give you a gift?" I don't know exactly what to give him. I only sense that I want to give him something. I reach into my heart and pull out a compass of shiny gold with a scroll design and a beautiful gold chain attached. It looks as if it came from the early twentieth century.

He receives the compass with a smile. Before leaving me, he gives some instructions. "This will help with direction for the area that runs along the north and south ends of Highway 95 from the top of the Lewiston Hill all the way up to the Canadian border. I coordinate with other angels. Now release me to go on to my next mission. You may call on my assistance at any time. You have authority over this land because you are functioning out of relationship with Yahweh."

What did I learn from this story?

Many of the events on this timeline happened just as I described them here. COVID-19 temporarily halted the construction phase of the highway. The lawsuit against the state was dismissed by the Ninth Circuit Court. City North American moved me. The door sheds were disassembled and arrived at my new home in a trailer. The neighbors across the street moved after I did, and the decrees and declarations happened in the manner I released them. Others who were displaced and did not come into alignment with the decrees and declarations had a difficult time with their relocation process. I found my new home and location to be more in line with my destiny than the home I lost.

This was the first time I saw how Yahweh's timeline works. This encounter occurred about one year prior to the offer for relocation presented to me by the state. I knew some of what I saw in the vision in the natural because I had read the Final Environmental Impact Statement. I knew the basic details of where the highway would go and what it might look like. I also understood some of the history of our region. But I had never experienced moving into the future and speaking life into it.

Angels are on assignment, and we have authority to release them into those assignments. When we speak with authority, they move. Until then, angels wait patiently for a Son of Yahweh to begin walking in his/her authority. When I stepped into my role for this project, the angelic showed up, and I partnered with them. Angels need the sons to release them to do their work.

I finally moved in the spring of 2019 to a completely new location three hours further north. I didn't understand why angels outside my actual city were even interested in this highway project and my relocation. I had no desire to move twenty minutes away, much less three hours. Had I known certain details earlier, I would not have been a happy camper. I was moved completely out of my comfort zone into a town I knew nothing about and had no job. I was alone, feeling quite clueless about any next steps. At my previous maturity level, that would have been a recipe for potential stress. As I walked through this process, I had plenty of practice learning to function from a place of rest in Christ. I learned to step into the unknown with an expectation that Yahweh would show me the next steps. And he did.

How did this story help with my personal great awakening?

New levels of authority and responsibility came out of this situation. My great awakening moved me into a new season. Subsequently, I realized the impact of the age we're entering when the lockdowns for COVID-19 began. Since we were all locked up in our homes, we had plenty of time for activations. I also stepped into another creative season. What the enemy meant for harm, Yahweh can turn into something good when people come into alignment with his intention.

What is our position? We can choose where to stand. Should the world circumstances dictate how we function? If we choose to accept that we're entering a new age that looks vastly different than what we could even think or expect, we stand a chance of participating in the building process. This includes seeing the body of Christ from a completely different perspective.

No expectations.

No preconceived ideas.

No fear.

Activation!

Take a current local, national, or world situation that's on your heart. Prophetically hold the situation in your hands and place them over your heart. Stay there until you feel at peace. Begin to see through Yahweh's eyes by visualizing yourself hovering above the earth as if you're in a spaceship looking through a window. As you hold the circumstance in your heart, wrap it in a blanket of love. I often release the blood of Yeshua into this love blanket so that it drips through the blanket into and through the entire circumstance. As you begin to engage with love, you may feel led to release decrees and declarations of truth, peace, righteousness, joy, understanding, unity, compassion, etc. A key here is to see an infusion of what you're releasing into the known and unknown details.

Next, in another prophetic act, see yourself standing in the heavenlies looking down over the circumstance. Take the love blanket dripping with the blood of Yeshua and release it from heaven into the earth directly into the situation. This brings the reality of what you've done from heaven into Earth. Set a continuous flow of Yahweh's love from your position in heaven.

What are your impressions? Journal what you see, sense, hear, and feel. Do you have a sense of what Yahweh wants to speak? If so, say it out loud. It's important to repeat a sequence frequently, sending waves of these spiritual goodies into any negative situation, because love covers all. No negative frequency can stand against love. Let's use Yahweh's sledgehammer of love to impact circumstances, situations, and conditions so they line up with Yahweh's truth, righteousness, and peace.

If a circumstance from the earthly perspective looks you in the eye, demanding your immediate attention, kick butt, take names, and tell it to take a hike. This is about our authority. Peace and rest are a great barometer for knowing when we're in Christ. When familiar spirits whisper sweet nothings in our ears, as our focus stays on Yeshua, negative junk doesn't stand a chance of bringing us into a place of fear, anxiety, or depression. In a nutshell, circumstances only rule us when we play with them. When we operate from a place of authority in heaven, we're functioning from a higher dimension. No adversary can touch us when we're seated in Christ.

This takes practice, patience, and perseverance. We do this in spite of how we feel or what we see. We simply exercise our authority by faith. We're learning to see from a different perspective than our natural point of view, which is incomplete.

POSTLUDE

Through my experiences in the heavenly realms, I learned to have confidence in the process of stepping into my sonship. Let's look again at the questions I introduce in the Prelude.

1) Do the details within the encounter line up with the character of Yahweh? I learned to recognize what came out of left field as a key in understanding Yahweh's character, that He was probably speaking to me, and that I should pay attention. Paradigms were shattered in the process, helping me to understand my authority in Christ.

2) Is what I'm seeing, sensing, hearing, and feeling bathed in Love? The Trinity is always gentle with me, like a good parent is with a child. I never felt made fun of, less than, or like I wasn't good enough. In fact, I felt edified, encouraged, and hungry for more.

3) Is anything required of me other than to love Yahweh and be loved by him? Even at times where I felt uncomfortable because my life circumstances were unprecedented, there was always a sense of peace. When I wasn't in a place of peace, Jesus grabbed my face and asked me to look into his eyes. I immediately felt peace return. His love resonated through my entire being and I eagerly responded.

4) Although a particular instance isn't in the Bible, do my encounters line up with Biblical principles? Prophecy is true if it comes to

pass, which is a Biblical principle. In the final chapter of the book where I'm hovering above the new highway, much of that vision has already transpired, confirming that what I saw was of Yahweh. It was totally off my grid and out of the context of my life; however, by that time in the relationship, my trust in the process of ascension was well established.

5) If something really doesn't make sense, when I look for any member of the Trinity in the experience, is one of them there? When I went to the beginning of time, Jesus was with me, which allowed me to feel comfortable about what I was experiencing. I also felt extreme peace and love emanating from him. It's important to pay attention to our emotions in the process. However, if we are in fear of being deceived, that will play into our reactions and how we perceive the experience. The more comfortable we are in our relationship with the Lord, the more confident we will become. The key here is to look for Jesus and have him walk you through the experience.

I had no idea that being displaced by a highway project was of Yahweh. In the past, considering a similar situation to be chaotic and a disruption in my life, my "go to" method was traditional spiritual warfare. In this case, I had seven years to discover Yahweh's will through ascension into the heavenlies, which superseded my own perceptions. As I walked out and exercised the authority Yahweh gave me as a Son, I brought peace to the land, was launched into a new season of my life, and began to participate in a creation and restoration process. Stepping into my mandate helped prepare me to function in the Age of Aquarius. Why is this important?

This progression of maturity solidified and established my personal relationship with the Lord. As I clean up the junk from my life, I'm launched into greater levels of authority. You see that develop throughout my stories. May this encourage you, too, as you become more intimate with The Trinity. It is a step-by-step process, which is important to remember. Think of it like moving from grade to grade in school. As I stated in the Prelude, Father enrolled me in Kingdom

School. In that school, there are always do-overs! Practice prepares you to move forward and it takes perseverance and patience.

At the end of the day, it is all about desire. What do you desire? Do you want a closer relationship with Yahweh, or do you just want the experience? I learned that when I enter an ascension with a desire to be with members of the Trinity – no strings attached – things happened because the experience was not the goal. Relationship is my goal. After all, it's all about love. The love frequency of Yahweh overrides anything negative. Yahweh has a unique love language for each of us. Every good and perfect gift comes from the Father of Lights. It's your turn to step into the ascension experience, which ultimately propels you into what is needed to function in the Age of Aquarius.

WHERE TO GET ASSISTANCE

The organizations listed below have interactive ascension groups where you can meet like-minded people. There are other great sources out there but if you want group interaction, these are the ones I'm most familiar with and trust.

NW Ekklesia (Northwest Ekklesia). The website is https://nwekklesia.com I'm part of this ekklesia as a member of the governmental team. We offer a monthly membership for a small fee, classes, mentoring sessions, and healing sessions. The monthly membership includes a weekly ascension group and special "members only" teachings. NW Ekklesia is a very relational group where people often get together in one another's homes.

Global Ascension International Network (GAIN). This group is facilitated by Nancy Coen and her daughter, Shannon Bates. They have weekly ascension groups and monthly teachings for a small monthly fee. Their website is: https://globalascensionnetwork.net/

Engaging Yahweh Programme through Freedom Arc. Mike Parsons runs this organization. For a small monthly fee, you have access to more teachings than you could possibly get through in two years. Upon request, you will be assigned to a mentoring group. That website is: https://eg.freedomarc.org/

Kingdom Equipping Center (KEC). Gil and Adena Hodges are the facilitators of this organization. They have many levels of participation and interaction. Everything they do is relational and interactive. Their website is: https://kingdomequippingcenter.com/

Further Reading

"Cosmic Shift — A New Season of Faith," by Christopher Paul Carter. The Fig and the Vine Publishing Company; Mount Pleasant, South Carolina: 2015. Christopher's book presents the details of the Great Year, Great Month and how the ages change. As a former high school science teacher, Christopher brings a Christian perspective into what many consider "new age" thought.

"Accessing Your Spiritual Inheritance," by Alice Briggs, Del Hungerford, and Seneca Schurbon. Kingdom Collective Publishers: 2016. This book walks you through understanding your spiritual inheritance and learning to take back what rightfully belongs to you and your generational line.

"Accessing the Kingdom Realms," by Del Hungerford. CreateSpace: 2017 In this book, I share experiences that helped me in the maturing process as a Son of God. He is faithful to lead us into greater intimacy with him. Out of that desire, I learned how to release what no longer served me.

Del's Websites

Healing Frequencies Music: https://www.healingfrequenciesmu-sic.com/ is the website where Del presents information on "all things frequency." In addition, all her music, books, and other materials are available for download. Her music is also available on iTunes, Amazon, and streaming services worldwide.

NW Ekklesia: https://nwekklesia.com/ is made up of people from the Pacific Northwest. They connect with ecclesiae around the world as well. NWE provides mentoring, classes, teachings, and opportunities for fellowship. Del is part of the Council of Seven that works together in governing the daily workings of the organization.

About the Author:

Del Hungerford is a musician, author, teacher, and business owner. She owns the recording label and business, Healing Frequencies Music. Her spontaneous instrumental music is intended to enhance cognitive function, heal the emotions, awaken intuition, and engage our senses. Del is a professional classical musician, published researcher, and teacher. Her presentation style invites students and readers to engage in the learning process through active participation. Her recent writings focus on developing deeper intimacy with Yahweh through stepping into the heavenly realms as a standard protocol for Christian living.

ENDNOTES

1. Bible Wheel. "Full Text Hebrew/Greek Bible Gematria Database, Rom. 8:19," accessed November 12, 2020, https://www.biblewheel.com/GR/GR_Database.php?b-num=45&cnum=8&vnum=19&SourceTxt=SCR&getverse=Go.
2. Bible Hub. Strong's Concordance, "575. apo," accessed December 17, 2020, https://biblehub.com/greek/575.htm.
3. Bible Hub. Strong's Concordance, "1380. dokeó," accessed December 17, 2020, https://biblehub.com/greek/1380.htm.
4. Bible Hub. Strong's Concordance, "2936. ktizó," accessed December 17, 2020, https://biblehub.com/greek/2936.htm.
5. Bible Hub. Strong's Concordance, "601. apokaluptó," accessed December 17, 2020, https://biblehub.com/greek/601.htm.
6. Bible Hub. Strong's Concordance, "5207. huios," accessed December 17, 2020, https://biblehub.com/greek/5207.htm,
7. Bible Wheel. "Full Text Hebrew/Greek Bible Gematria Database, Gen. 1:28," accessed November 12, 2020, https://www.biblewheel.com/GR/GR_Database.php?b-num=1&cnum=1&vnum=28&SourceTxt=SCR&getverse=Go.
8. Open Stax, "U.S. History, 4.4 Great Awakening and Enlightenment," accessed November 19, 2020, https://open-stax.org/books/us-history/pages/4-4-great-awakening-and-enlightenment.
9. The Great Year. "Home," accessed November 22, 2020, https://thegreatyear.com.

10. Frances Rolleston, Mazzoroth: The Constellations, Including Mizraim, Astronomy of Egypt, (York Beach: Maine: Weiser Books, 2001), https://books.google.com/books?id=wR-kxMYF3k0C&source=gbs_similarbooks.

11. Wikipedia, s.v. "Outline of wars," last modified December 2, 2020, https://en.wikipedia.org/wiki/Outline_of_war#Wars.

12. Wikipedia, s.v. "List of epidemics," last modified December 17, 2020, https://en.wikipedia.org/wiki/List_of_epidemics.

13. Wikipedia, s.v. "List of famines," last modified, December 12, 2020, https://en.wikipedia.org/wiki/List_of_famines.

14. Wikipedia, s.v. "List of droughts," last modified, December 8, 2020, https://en.wikipedia.org/wiki/List_of_droughts.

15. Wikipedia, s.v. "List of earthquakes," last modified, December 12, 2020, https://en.wikipedia.org/wiki/Lists_of_earthquakes.

16. Wikipedia, s.v. "List of large volcanic eruptions," last modified, December 16, 2020, https://en.wikipedia.org/wiki/List_of_large_volcanic_eruptions.

17. Wikipedia, s.v. "List of volcanic eruptions by death toll," last modified, December 17, 2020, https://en.wikipedia.org/wiki/List_of_volcanic_eruptions_by_death_toll.

18. The majority of sources came from Wikipedia because they provide comprehensive lists of these types of events. Other sources were pieced together for the droughts from the Encyclopedia Britannica and Wikipedia. As scientists continue to research ancient civilization, additional events will probably be discovered.

19. Wikipedia, s.v. "Timeline of the 18th century," last modified, August 25, 2020, https://en.wikipedia.org/wiki/Timeline_of_the_18th_century.

20. Wikipedia, s.v. "Great Awakening," last modified, November 25, 2020, https://en.wikipedia.org/wiki/Great_Awakening.

21. Healing Frequencies Music, "Home," accessed November 26, 2020, https://www.healingfrequenciesmusic.com/product/waves-spirit-full-album-download.

22. Kenneth E. Hagin, Why Tongues? (Tulsa: Kenneth Hagin Ministries, 2001).

23. Healing Frequencies, https://healingfrequenciesmusic.com.

24. Freedom Flowers, "Home," accessed December 17, 2020, https://www.freedom-flowers.com/divine-sound-essences.

25. Bible Wheel. "Full Text Hebrew/Greek Bible Gematria Database, Gen. 30:39," accessed November 21, 2020, https://www.biblewheel.com/GR/GR_Database.php?bnum=1&cnum=30&vnum=39&getverse=Go.